T0244597

Renewing
New Testament
Christology

LEANDER E. KECK

Renewing
New Testament
Christology

Foreword
DAVID KECK

Afterword
RICHARD B. HAYS

Fortress Press
Minneapolis

RENEWING NEW TESTAMENT CHRISTOLOGY

Library of Congress Control Number: 2023933513 (print)

Cover image: The Resurrection of Christ, 15th century, Giovanni Dal Ponte (Giovanni di Marco), Tempera on poplar panel
Cover design: Savanah N. Landerholm

Print ISBN: 978-1-5064-9376-3
eBook ISBN: 978-1-5064-9377-0

To
Ann T. Keck
and
Prue and Bob Morgan

A modern philosopher [and theologian] who has never once suspected himself as a charlatan must be such a shallow mind that his work is probably not worth reading.

Leszek Kolakowski

CONTENTS

FOREWORD

David Keck

When my father said that he would discard all the previous manuscripts of this book once we had completed reviewing the page proofs, I asked him to wait, saying simply, "They are an embodiment of *Taking the Bible Seriously*," his first book.

As his editor for the last several years, I had seen many revisions to chapters, paragraphs, sentences, and words—a seemingly endless quest to say what could be said about New Testament Christology the best possible way. He has been laboring on this project for over 50 years, and there have been times when it seemed like health issues would prevent its completion. Not wanting this to be a posthumous publication, I did not always respond well when he sent me (once again) additional hand-written pages and corrections to a chapter that I thought he had finished.

Ultimately, however, I came to respect the fact that his constant revisiting of ideas and their expression was a model for how to listen to Scripture.

The word "seriously" appears not just in the title of his first book, but it appears throughout his writing. This book is the product of taking the Bible seriously throughout his life, something every generation needs to learn to do. An adverb, not a noun or a verb, "seriously" characterizes a way of attending to Scripture, a disciplined orientation and attitude.

Taking New Testament Christology seriously has meant for him a persistent striving to listen to what the New Testament writers are actually saying. Not what he thinks they say, not what he wants them to say, not what ecclesiastical statements, pastors, or scholars say they say, but what they themselves say in their own terms. It entails learning to think with them, to let their thinking shape ours.

To be sure, the Christian tradition has guided his reading, shaping his questions and providing conversation partners, but to him the New Testament remains—even after decades of study—mysterious, challenging, puzzling, potent, surprising, and life-giving. See the epigraph he provided for this book for a poignant insight into his thinking about his life's work.

Watching him over these years has made me realize how unserious my own reading of the Bible can be.

How often has a confessional statement, political agenda, scholarly trend, or church fundraising campaign predetermined what I think Scripture is saying? How often have I unconsciously treated a passage as a convenient tool (or even weapon) for a worthy goal? Taking the Bible seriously does not mean using or deploying it frivolously. It means instead abiding in this humbling reality: Scripture relativizes, even judges us and all our efforts.

With Scripture as in life, the worst listeners are the ones who already know what is being said.

I hesitate to go back over my sermons to see how often I knew what the sermon would be about before even reading the pericope. Or how often I have "studied" the passage only to confirm my point of view while overlooking something challenging.

How frequently did I choose to focus on the more comforting verses of a passage (and quietly hoped that the congregation wouldn't ask about the awkward parts)? High praise from my father after a sermon: "The pastor didn't shy away from the text's difficulties."

Most pastors, perhaps, develop a picture of Jesus derived primarily from one Gospel and supplemented by the others. The Lukan Jesus's concern for the poor is the essential Jesus, and it just so happens that he is incarnate Logos. They are the same person, after all. But one of the clearest implications of this book is not to preach unwittingly about the Jesus presented in Luke when preaching on a passage in

Matthew. Taking this book seriously means respecting the contrasts and even conflicts between the New Testament writers—and struggling with this messy reality given to us in the canon.

This book challenges the unserious, albeit understandable tendency to simplify and neatly synthesize the New Testament to satisfy our agendas. On many occasions, my father has mentioned in passing the fact that the early church rejected Tatian's attempt in the second century to create one synthesized Gospel out of the four. The level of respect he has for that ecclesial decision—especially given how much more complicated as well as richer that decision makes the theological disciplines—probably cannot be overstated.

Taking the Bible seriously means that one does not sit in judgment over it or pick and choose as convenient. Instead, it begins with the theological discipline of respect, a respect akin to Simone Weil's description of prayer as rapt attention. Such respect contrasts with a fundamentalist's devoted worship of the Bible (which can become its own form of knowing what the Bible says in advance). How did he develop this respect? A few words on my father's upbringing and professional development are in order.

My father is a peasant who became the Dean of Yale Divinity School but never forgot that he was a peasant.

He comes by his peasantness the only way one can—honestly. One of his mentors, Erich Dinkler, commented to my father after shaking hands with my grandfather, "Your father is a real peasant." A polite American speaker would have used "farmer," but the word Dinkler chose as a German speaker was accurate in referring to the strong, thick hands of someone who had worked a farm all his life, hauled 10-gallon milk pails up a hill to be sold when that could earn some money, and even labored for a logging company to feed his family and support his church. Before going to college, my father did many of these things by his side, also working in a lumber mill.

Similarly, my father's mother was a no-nonsense, faithful woman who told him Bible stories before the days of radio. He remembers a formative exegetical principle of hers, "If I don't understand what something means, I just leave it alone." At an early age, he learned that the Bible is something greater than we are, something to be listened to seriously. We are not to fill in meaning or provide answer for the sake of having answers.

In a 1968 Advent sermon delivered at Vanderbilt Divinity School and published in his *Echoes of the Word*, my father refers to Christian leaders who grew up in circumstances very much like his who "find that we can enjoy Jack Daniels as we consort with the establishment, and cannot get over the wonder of it all" (183–84).

He was, I believe, remembering where he came from amid the temptations of social mobility and status. In our world of increasing economic opportunities and technological developments, it is easy for Scripture's readers to get caught up in "the wonder of it all" while missing the wonder of Scripture.

Recently, he commented on his formation as a peasant— "Peasants aren't responsible for society, they are just trying to make the best of whatever tough circumstances they are in." Consequently, while my father has been respectful of the claims of the Social Gospel, he has always seen his essential task as discerning the wonder of Scripture and to honor the way *that* wonder and its audacious claims encourage, challenge, comfort, judge, liberate, and even save.

Taking the Bible seriously entails locating the concerns of contemporary politics in the larger framework of Scripture's own claims. As will be seen in the book, he argues that the New Testament writers are less concerned about our issues than we want them to be. And he trusts that this is a good thing. By inviting us into a reality greater than we can conceive, Scripture does speak to humanity's persistent suffering, giving the hope-filled courage needed to endure and serve through times of uncertainty, violence, and disease.

In his peasant upbringing, my father saw the power of the Gospel in his own home and surrounding community. Remembering that the power of God produces generosity, devotion, and hope in households with very little money or formal education instills an extraordinary respect for the Bible.

At the same time, he also discovered that scholarship was a way of opening up the riches of Scripture. He remains indebted to liberal Protestant theology, which he first encountered at Linfield College. It freed him from some of the constrictions of his peasant framework and drew his attention seriously to the teachings of Jesus. At Andover Newton seminary, he learned from Paul Minear the importance of apocalyptic for the New Testament. While apocalyptic thinking can legitimate terrible violence, taking apocalyptic seriously can also mean relativizing one's own agendas and efforts, thereby liberating the reader to attend to what Scripture is actually saying, what *God* is actually doing.

He grew up in a German-speaking household, and this facilitated his graduate study at Yale and in Germany during the post-war years. Two of his mentors had been drafted by the Nazis. One suffered for five years in a Soviet POW camp, and the other, Ernst Käsemann, suffered imprisonment for preaching against the regime. Faithful exegesis of the New Testament was an urgent need for Germany in the 1950s (as it had been in the 1930s, alas), and studying in this context certainly underscored the imperative to take the Bible seriously.

As a faculty member at Vanderbilt, Emory, and Yale, he co-taught with faculty in almost all the other theological disciplines. He was convinced that the Bible had something important to say and that he had something important to learn from his colleagues, particularly those who became close friends. Taking Scripture seriously entailed for him a willingness to explore important topics together. Similarly, he committed himself to writing for the church, contributing to curricular projects such as the Disciple Bible Study program, as well as to resources for pastoral leaders, such as the New Interpreters Bible. Taking the Bible seriously has meant taking the church seriously, too. Although he developed intellectually beyond his peasant background and was well placed to share a Jack Daniels or two, he never forgot that the Gospel has transformative power for all who receive it seriously, regardless of education or social status.

He remembers wryly what a lay-pastor studying at Vanderbilt once said to him: "I preached better before I took your course." My father had made the study of the New Testament more complex, more problematic, and the student was wrestling with what happens when you find that the Bible is not what you thought it was growing up. My father had gone through this process himself in college—only he found it invigorating. Looking back on his teaching he expressed another aspect of what it means to take the New Testament seriously, "You need to learn to think the way it thinks, to ask the questions it asks, to listen to what it is actually saying." This book refers to the audacity of Scripture—the bold, bracing claims it makes about God, Jesus, humanity. Those who think they already know what Scripture says may preach more fluently, but they may miss this audacity.

My father fondly remembers singing—both Sunday-night hymn sings growing up and the times at the Society of Biblical Literature when he and his colleagues would start singing some of the old hymns and gospel songs they all grew up with. Such music gave melody, harmony, and rhythm to the images from Scripture they shared. Shall we gather at the River? Taking the Bible seriously entails respect for the myriad ways it shapes communities.

Singing may also serve as a metaphor for taking the Bible seriously. Singing in a group means listening to multiple voices, both as individual voices and in their shared harmonies and dissonances. In a way, my father's reading of New Testament Christology resembles listening to a choir. Instead of expecting 27 voices in perfect unison (or forcing them to sing in unison), he listens to multiple voices moving in various ways all at once, ever trusting that the whole is not just more beautiful but more holy. Painful truths can perhaps be expressed—and experienced—more honestly through dissonance.

Ultimately, this book explores some of the underlying logic and implications of the "already-not yet" way of thinking. Already God's decisive work has begun, but it is not yet completed. Taking the Bible seriously for my father has involved taking the already-not yet seriously.

That is, in the present moment there is a divine reality at work and we are compelled to respond, all the while remembering that this is not the final, ultimate moment, and that all our readings remain provisional.

Hence, the need to read and reread, write, and rewrite. And just when you think you have the sentence right, rewrite it again because it is not quite right. Yet. It is this process of faithful scholarship that I hope this Foreword provides some witness to.

My father once described his experience of faith: "At a young age, Jesus grabbed a hold of me and never let me go." After more than 50 years of working on *Renewing New Testament Christology*, it is fair to say that my father returned the favor.

PREFACE

This book redefines "New Testament Christology" as both content (what the NT says about Christ) and as the scholarly discipline that explains that content. Behind this dual redefinition stands a particular conviction: Instead of perpetuating the prevailing view of NT Christology as a theologically informed *history* of early Christian ideas about Christ, one should see it as a historically informed theological discourse. The goal of the current view is an accurate, theologically literate construction of past beliefs about Christ. The advocated alternative seeks to understand the logic, the reasoning, that makes NT assertions about Christ intelligible parts of a coherent whole. This formulation distills the result of the book's own complex, five-decade-long history. A word about that history seems appropriate at the outset.

The Book's Biography

The 1969 lectures titled "The Man Jesus in the New Testament," given at the theological college of the University of Winnipeg, began this book. Instead of probing the extent to which the Christology of Matthew, John, Romans, and Hebrews is traceable to Jesus's self-interpretation (still debated today) or analyzing how each writer construed the Christological titles (e.g., Christ, Son of Man) he used to interpret Jesus (a common procedure at the time), I sought to grasp each writing's Christology as the core of a coherent theological understanding of the Jesus event as a whole. This made soteriology—the view of salvation—the heart of Christology's subject matter.[1] In subsequent seminars, public lectures, and sundry publications, the material was repeatedly expanded and contracted, revised and rewritten, set aside and taken up again—and finally turned into the manuscript for this book. In the process, the book's agenda and its significance for a wider readership became increasingly clear.

Completing the present manuscript was delayed repeatedly, partly by personal circumstances, partly by various professional responsibilities. Though publishing[2] and lecturing in various venues diverted energy from the Christology project itself, they also sharpened the argument and encouraged its somewhat oral style. One lecture was especially significant: "Toward the Renewal of the New Testament Christology," given at the annual meeting of Studiorum Novi Testamentum Societas in Trondheim, Norway, in 1981.[3] While many endowed lectureships do not require publication, I regard this book as the published form of the following: The Shaffer Lectures (Yale, 1980), McFadin Lectures (Texas Christian University, 1986), Cole Lectures (Vanderbilt Divinity School, 1987), Speaker's Lectures (Oxford University), and Stone Lectures (Princeton Theological Seminary), both in 2005.

The final revision was, however, arrested twice, once by a stroke in 2019 that impaired my vision and hampered my writing ability (never exemplary) and once by Covid whose aftermath sapped my strength. Completing the manuscript seemed beyond my reach. But unexpectedly, the improbable became possible. With the assistance of David Keck and Richard B. Hays, the support of Carey Newman at Fortress Press, and the marvels of electronic communication, I was able to complete the manuscript in a few months. I remain deeply indebted to these colleagues. Without their aid, this book would not exist.

Chapter 5 was completed and chapter 6 extensively revised. Chapter 4 (a Stone Lecture) was left unchanged. David Keck and Richard Hays have generously provided the Foreword and Afterword, respectively.

The Book's Rationale

Advocating NT Christology as a historically informed theological enterprise readily suggested the book's two-part structure: the treatment of the four Christologies in Part 2 is warranted by the arguments in Part 1. Its first chapter neither surveys nor summarizes the history of research but instead sees historical criticism's dominance in Christian theology as a whole in the light of the modern "history of history"; it also notes the consequences for Christology. The chapter is not an abbreviated history of modern Christian thought, but an historically informed argument about the impact of "history" on Christology.

Chapter 2 provides a crisp *formal* statement of Christology's task as the clue to its nature. By approaching Christology functionally— by grasping what it does and how it does it—and by understanding its logic, one can grasp its character generically before examining the *material* content of any particular Christology. For the redefinition of NT Christology advocated here, understanding Christology generically is more important than seeing a given Christology genetically— that is, in terms of its antecedents. Christology's logic, its reasoning, is especially important here, for it accounts for the way Jesus's religious significance—however construed—is grounded in his relation to God. Finally, the chapter's precise definition of *New Testament* Christology accounts for the largely exegetical character of the book's second part.

In Part 2, the approach outlined in the second chapter is applied to two Gospels (Matthew and John) and two Epistles (Romans and Hebrews). These four chapters can be read in any sequence because their order is not part of the argument. Simply juxtaposing these chapters allows each voice to be heard in its own register. Part 2 shuns talking of NT Christology's "unity" (sometimes a mischievous word) without thereby doubting that the NT's diverse Christologies also share certain ways of thinking, expressed in differing words. Showing this, however, is not this book's task.

As the expanding and contracting, the including and the excluding, continued, it became ever more essential to stay focused on what must be said and thereby omit what was not necessary, though important, informative, or interesting. To facilitate comprehension, higher priority was given to clarity, precision, and conciseness than to completeness.

Largely absent, therefore, are discussions that compare or contrast the four Christologies with those of other early Christian texts (extant or inferred), as well as with Greco-Roman religious ideas. It is doubtful whether dealing also with such matters would have made the argument stronger or more convincing.

Since my quarrel was with the prevailing view of NT Christology, not with my colleagues' particular judgments or interpretations, there is no need to record my agreements and dissents or to comment on everything I have read for this project. Doing so would have detracted from the argument itself. Accordingly, footnotes are rare in Part 2, and the bibliography identifies only what has been cited.

Part 1

FINDING THE RIGHT SUBJECT

⟨ 1 ⟩

CHANGING THE SUBJECT

NEW TESTAMENT CHRISTOLOGY did not become the history of early Christology by accident. It was rather part of the general mutation of NT theology into the history of early Christianity that William Wrede (1859–1906) explicitly called for in 1897. Since the present book claims that the renewal of NT Christology, as both subject matter and discipline, entails a change of direction, this chapter's first aim is to hear carefully what Wrede called for and to note what happened as a result. Its second task is to understand why he was followed so widely. The third is to identify some of the consequences of transforming a theological discipline into an historical one—in other words, the results of changing NT Christology's subject matter.

Instead of Doctrine

In Wrede's eyes, the discipline of NT theology—of which Christology is the pivotal part—is to be "totally indifferent to all dogmatic and systematic theology." Indeed, "how the systematic theologian gets on with the results [of describing early Christianity historically] . . . is his own affair." In saying such things, Wrede was not venting his personal alienation from Christian doctrine; in his mind he was guarding his vision of NT theology against theology's distorting influence that he saw in current treatments of NT theology. If his objections were valid, a viable alternative cannot ignore them; it must absorb them while not being immobilized by them.

The Pivotal Critique
In a vacation course for pastors, Wrede declared current forms of NT theology bankrupt and outlined his vision of its proper task.[1] Wrede's

main target was the critically conservative work by Bernhard Weiss (1827–1918), *The Biblical Theology of the New Testament.*[2] Wrede found four flaws in this influential work: (a) It "does considerable violence" to the NT by emphasizing "doctrinal concepts" (73–84, *Lehrbegriffe*) because writings like 1 Peter or James are "simply too small to extract doctrinal positions from." (b) Doctrine itself is rare in the NT, most of which consists of "practical advice . . . [and] the stirring up of religious feelings"; therefore, the prevailing method epitomized by Weiss "makes doctrine out of what in itself is not doctrine and fails to bring out what it really is"—evidence of early Christian religion. (c) In treating each writing's concepts exhaustively, Weiss's method becomes "the science of minutiae," thereby losing "the living freshness" of the NT, a product of vital early Christian religion. (d) Even if presented in proper chronological sequence, Weiss's "little biblical theologies" do not "show us the special character of early Christian ideas and perceptions, sharply profiled," and so do not help us to understand them historically"—that is, as "a true reproduction of early Christian religion and theology."[3] In short, what is called "New Testament theology" is "wrong in both its terms" because it mislabels the real subject matter, "the history of early Christian religion and theology" (116).

From Wrede's perspective, the nature of the NT writings itself disallowed Weiss's method and resisted Weiss's inevitably wrong results because doctrinal concepts (*Lehrbegriffe*) obscure the NT's purpose, viz, bolstering the emerging Christian religion. Getting at that called for a completely different approach. Moreover, in solely describing the past and so avoiding doctrine, the historian had no responsibility for safeguarding the church's theological and religious heritage. Thus when Wrede rejected this role as beyond the discipline's capacity (72–73), he disengaged NT theology—as discipline and subject matter—from deliberate, explicit participation in the life of the church.[4] What sort of role this envisioned history of early Christianity could, or should, play in current church life Wrede did not say. It was not his business to say.

The Envisioned Alternative

Wrede boldly summoned fellow NT scholars toward one goal alone, *"the history of early Christian religion"* (89, italics added), to about 150 CE, to be portrayed "as objectively, correctly and sharply as possible. That is all . . . Like every other science, New Testament theology has its goal simply in itself, and is totally indifferent to all dogmatic and systematic theology." Wrede's goal is an accurate description of *"what was believed, thought, required and striven for . . . not what certain writings say about faith, doctrine, hope, etc."* (84, his italics). The investigator "must be guided by a pure disinterested concern for knowledge" and so bracket out one's "own viewpoint, however precious. Then indeed he will know only what really was" (70).[5]

Wrede said more about transforming the discipline than about the subject matter's content, for he was not setting out in advance the results of his redefined discipline but stating his guiding principles. Two of them have been taken for granted for years: first, writing the history of the early Christian religion requires using *all* the Christian sources from the period, not simply the NT. Further, all sources of information must be treated equally because, for the historian, the canonical status of the NT is irrelevant. Second, one "should . . . make clear . . . the development and developments that were important historically" (91). Individual writers who did not have "an epoch-making influence on the church" (85) were to take a back seat, not given equal attention. In other words, "the procedure is always *genetic and comparative*" (96, italics added), for only so could the important developments be identified and explained.

The genetic procedure implies that the history of the Christian religion must begin with Jesus's preaching, which, however, "cannot be presented as an actual doctrine" (*Lehrbegriff*), for it "cannot be cut loose from Jesus's personality, and the course of his life, so far as this can be known"; indeed, "neither his proclamation of the kingdom of God nor even his preaching of true righteousness is independent of his 'plan,' his understanding of his vocation." Consequently, "Jesus's own world of ideas must be reproduced" by the historian.[6]

Partly in light of Paul, but especially because "we do not possess *ipsissima verba* of Jesus," the comparative procedure is essential because the presentation "must at every decisive point first distinguish between what is original and what has come later" (103–4). However limited our knowledge of the early church, its Jewish-Christian faith must be distinguished from Christianity on *heathen* soil." Beyond doubt, Paul is "*the* epoch-making figure in the history of primitive Christianity," and so "the creator of a Christian theology" (106). Still, "Paul is being considered here, not for his own sake but as a member of a historical sequence" (107). Actually, Wrede emphasized the Apostle's "very wide distance from Jesus." Indeed, "nobody can write a New Testament theology as the development and continuation of Jesus's teaching . . . it is an absolutely essential task to investigate the *historical* relationship of Paul to Jesus, to measure the distance between them and, so far as one can, explain it" (108, italics added). Wrede's influential *Paulus* (1907) will call the Apostle "the second founder of Christianity."

Wrede's reliance on the genetic and comparative becomes concrete particularly in his insistence that (a) "Judaism, not the Old Testament, is the basis of Christianity in the history of religion" (114), (b) that Johannine theology is to be understood in light of a pre-Christian gnosticism (111),[7] and (c) that the growing dogmatization of the original picture of the life of Jesus can be demonstrated from the gospels. In a lapidary sentence that anticipates both form and redaction criticism, Wrede adds, "What critical procedures cut out as not an authentic part of Jesus's preaching is now—with other material—evaluated constructively to depict the emergence of the gospel picture of Jesus." In other words, the gospels may tell us more about early Christianity than about Jesus himself.

Wrede harbored no second thoughts. Six years after *Task and Method*, he addressed The New Theology Society in Breslau on the topic "Theological Study and the History of Religion," in which he called for "the *transformation* of the customary and . . . untenable discipline of New Testament theology into the history of early Christian religion and theology" (italics added). He himself could not carry out what he envisaged and called for because early death (at 47) cut short his remarkably provocative career.

The Alternative Achieved

What Wrede called for, however, was produced in exemplary fashion by Wilhelm Bousset (1865–1920),[8] whose magisterial *Kyrios Christos* appeared in 1913 (ET 1970), subtitled "A History of Belief in Christ from the Beginnings of Christianity to Irenaeus." Although the phrase *kyrios christos* appears in the NT only in 1 Peter 3:15, for Bousset it expressed a major feature of early Christianity, especially beyond Palestine: "Jesus of Nazareth in essence as the Lord of the community, venerated in the cultus." Bousset emphasized religion experienced in communal worship, as allegedly found also in certain non-Christian groups he also studied. Thus he claimed to have eliminated "the separation of the religious history of primitive Christianity from the general development of the religious life surrounding Christianity" (13); overcoming this separation was the heart of the agenda of the "History of Religion School" (see below).

Bousset, convinced that "in its beginning . . . Christianity has nothing, nothing at all, to do with the philosophical literature of the educated circles" (15), situated the Christianity that took root beyond Palestine within the general syncretistic religiosity of ordinary folk. Drawing on the work of classicists like Richard Reizenstein as well as on his own research,[9] he found in early Christianity's environment "a strange world of its own with a special and unmistakable structure" that "quite early merged with the gospel of Jesus" (21), thereby forming a Christianity that differed markedly from the original in Jerusalem (as Wrede had noted). For Bousset, the hellenization of Christianity was pivotal: "No other event even approaches this in importance . . . and . . . Christology represents the center of the whole development" (11–12). Christians did not decide to "borrow" ideas and practices from the syncretized religious world (as some scholars were saying); rather, "the most important appropriation [the worship of Jesus in the cultus and the two sacraments] . . . is more an unconscious process in the life of the community" (21).

Combining rhetorical skill and religious sensibility, Bousset described a hellenistic congregation's cultic worship of the Lord Jesus in a passage that deserves to be quoted more fully:

> *Around the* kyrios *the community is gathered in believing
> reverence. It confesses his name, under the invocation of
> his name it baptizes, it assembles around the table of the
> Lord Jesus; to the Lord . . . already now the first day of the
> week is dedicated . . . under the invocation of his name
> people perform miracles and drive demons out! . . . In the
> gathering of the fellowship, in worship and in cult, there
> grew up . . . the consciousness of their unity . . . abandoned to
> scorn and contempt, they came together in the evening . . . for
> the common sacred meal. There they expressed the miracle of
> fellowship, the glow of enthusiasm of a common faith and
> a common hope; there the spirit blazed high and a world
> full of wonders surrounded them; prophets and those who
> speak in tongues, visionaries and ecstatic persons begin to
> speak; psalms, hymns and spiritual songs sound through the
> room . . . And over this whole swaying sea of inspiration
> reigns the Lord Jesus as the head of the community, with his
> power immediately present in breathtaking palpable presence
> and certainty.* (134–35)

Meanwhile, back in Palestine, Christianity was a modified Jewish religion: "In Jesus's preaching, and in that of the primitive community, the simple idea of forgiveness of sins plays a central and dominant role, and . . . there are perfected here . . . the Old Testament religion and particularly . . . the religion of late Judaism." In Palestinian Christianity, "not even the slightest trace is found of the supernaturalism of the Pauline religion of redemption" (182) thus agreeing with Wrede's *Paulus*. Palestinian Christianity focused on Jesus as the Son of Man, expected to come from heaven as the Judge—a view that did not come from Jesus but was attributed to him by the earliest church and that manifests the influence of the ancient myth of the primal human, the *Urmensch* (see below).

One can hardly overemphasize the influence of Bousset's book in the transformation of NT Christology.[10] Having no real rival, its bold account of early Christology was both comprehensive in its range and thorough in its integration of vast learning (not only Bousset's) with religious sensibility. By distinguishing earliest (Jewish) Palestinian Christianity from rapidly hellenized (gentile) Christianity beyond Palestine, Bousset created a construction that could not be ignored. He did not need to disdain doctrine, as did Wrede; he either bypassed it or absorbed it into his warm, empathetic portrayal of early Christian religion in its two-stage development.

But Bousset's construction could not endure for long. As the extensive hellenization of Palestinian Jewry became ever more obvious, Bousset's simple contrast was greatly modified or widely abandoned. Scholars detected an intermediate Christianity formed among hellenized Jews (a hellenistic Jewish Christianity), within Palestine itself and elsewhere (e.g., Damascus). Nonetheless, his view affected profoundly the study of NT Christology. For one thing, by using Bousset's construction to distinguish the Jesus traditions formed in (and by) hellenistic Christianity from those developed earlier in Palestine, Bultmann's *History of the Synoptic Tradition* not only reduced markedly the quantity of Jesus traditions that could be considered genuine, but also allowed historians to see the nongenuine materials in the gospels as primary sources for the history of early Christology (as Wrede foresaw). Also, the structure of Bultmann's landmark *New Testament Theology* follows that of Bousset's *Kyrios Christos*.

In addition—and perhaps more significant in the long run—Bousset gave the "hellenization of Christianity" a positive interpretation. In his eyes, this development, discussed since the time of Erasmus and Melanchthon,[11] was not the corrupter of the true Christian religion taught by Jesus, as it was for the seventeenth-century anti-Trinitarians, eighteenth-century Enlightenment anti-Christian polemicists, and those who traced the objectionable in Catholicism to the intrusion of Greek and Roman paganism. Instead, it was Christianity's natural development as it grew beyond its homeland. Bousset's view, despite its oversimplification, was a clear advance beyond that of Adolf von Harnack (1851–1930), who regarded hellenization as the second-century influence of Greek culture (primarily philosophy) that furnished the Christian mind with "quite foreign presuppositions"—in particular "the hellenic idea that knowledge coincides with the essence of faith itself."[12] For von Harnack, "dogma in its conception and development is the work of the Greek spirit on the soil of the Gospel" (17), and the second-century gnostic systems were "the acute secularizing or hellenizing of Christianity" (227).[13]

It was through Bousset's history of early Christian belief in Christ that Wrede's vision had its most enduring impact. Some scholars questioned details while accepting the larger picture, as did Shirley Jackson Case at Chicago, for instance;[14] others rejected the whole construction, as did Princeton Seminary's J. Gresham Machen[15] and Berlin's church historian Karl Holl,[16] while the British Rawlinson engaged its implications for NT Christology in his 1926 Bampton Lectures, "The New Testament Doctrine of Christ." The result, however, was essentially the same: a debate over the correctness or adequacy of virtually every aspect of the constructed past of Christianity, especially over "what was believed, thought, taught, hoped, required, and striven for" (to use Wrede's language). In other words, the more Bousset's critics and supporters focused on the *history* of beliefs about Christ, the more the history of beliefs replaced the logic of belief, thereby abandoning *Christology*, as we will see. But first we must understand why the transformation of NT Christology into the history of early Christology was so attractive.

The Lure of History

The 1896 meeting of theologians associated with the liberal periodical *Die Christliche Welt* (comparable to *The Christian Century*) was startled when a brash young man, only two years into his first professorship, sprang to the platform and announced, "Gentlemen, *Alles wackelt*" (everything is tottering), then left the room, slamming the door behind him.[17] Thus, Ernst Troeltsch (1865–1923) disclosed the gap between his perception of Christianity's status and theirs.

The books by Wrede and Bousset appeared in this turbulent milieu characterized by the unevenly accelerating disintegration of Christendom—the symbiotic relation between the Christian religion and its cultural context in the West,[18] whether encoded in law or crystallized in custom and habits of thought. Neither the various renewal movements (e.g., Pietism in Germany, the Tractarians at Oxford, or the "Awakenings" in America) nor the rejuvenation sparked by aggressive "foreign missions" arrested the relentless erosion of Christendom.[19] As the "secularization" (not a helpful word)[20] proceeded, Christianity decreasingly provided a common conceptual framework and language. In addition, given the church's diverse historic roles in Christianizing European peoples,[21] modern upheavals—scientific, socioeconomic, political as well as religious—repeatedly diminished loyalty to the Christian religion and fostered outright hostility as well. The complex story of the West's dechristianization has been told repeatedly; it need not be summarized or surveyed again here. A few vivid details suffice to recall what was going on.

Beginning with the late eighteenth century, some intellectuals turned to a virtual paganism.[22] Heinrich Heine (1797–1856) foresaw the day when the influence of the cross on Germans "will break into miserable fragments. The old stone gods will arise . . . and wipe the dust of a thousand years from their eyes." No nineteenth-century figure repudiated Christianity more vehemently than Friedrich Nietzsche (1844–1900). At the end of *The Antichrist,* written against the Christian church, came the most terrible charge any prosecutor has ever uttered: Christianity is "the *one* great curse, the *one* great intrinsic depravity . . . the *one* immortal blemish of mankind (his italics)." Not accidentally, Peter Gay's *The Enlightenment* is subtitled "The Rise of Modern Paganism." The preface notes that "theirs was a paganism directed against their Christian inheritance and depended upon the paganism of classical antiquity," though modernized.

The more Christianity was put on the defensive and lost confidence in the metaphysical bases of its beliefs, the more Christian thought looked to history to ground a Christian faith that was to be intellectually secure and religiously energizing. Conservatives and liberals alike expected history to provide doubt-dissolving, confidence-building evidence—the former hoping to confirm a somewhat chastened orthodox tradition, the latter seeking to legitimate both their emancipation from it and their revisionist alternatives for it. Not surprisingly, then, it was the liberals who welcomed the transformation of NT Christology into the history of the early Christian religion. They were dissatisfied with the efforts of "mediating theologians" to make inherited beliefs more credible piecemeal, and so found Wrede's program attractive and Bousset's portrayal persuasive, for both views rode the wave of scientific history.[23] This massive, unprecedented appeal to history was the context in which Wrede's program and Bousset's achievement were either appropriated or resisted. The rest of this chapter therefore identifies, all too briefly, what was entailed in this apologetic reliance on history, and some of the consequences for the study of NT Christology.

History's Appeal

In the nineteenth century, the study of history ceased to be a hobby of learned gentlemen and became a *scientific discipline,*[24] sailing the flag of "objectivity."[25] "Historian" became a profession. In the twentieth century, the profession's growth was explosive: someone calculated that there were more historians at work in the 1980s than in the total number from Herodotus to 1960.[26] It was Leopold von Ranke (1795–1886) who, more than any other historian, facilitated the new era in historiography. His Berlin research seminar trained young scholars in the critical use of official documents, often long sequestered in archives, to *narrate* the past *wie es eigentlich gewesen* [*ist*] (how it actually was).[27] Ranke himself had no formal training as a historian, but he had a predecessor in Barthold G. Niebuhr (1776–1831), whose important history of Rome he read.[28] Niebuhr's self-confidence presaged that of the emerging profession: "I am a historian, for I can make a complete picture from separate fragments, and I know where the missing parts are and how to fill them up" (quoted by Gooch, 19)—many scholars writing the life of Jesus thought the same!

At Göttingen, chairs in history were created in the latter half of the eighteenth century.[29] With this institutional base, copied elsewhere, historians became academics, setting standards of the profession for which they became gatekeepers through faculty appointments. German historians created a formidable history industry, using as raw materials both newly found evidence (material and textual) and newly produced critical editions of texts. The scope and bulk of their publications, ranging from technical articles to monographs to encyclopedias to popular pieces, is astounding. To the "history of history" (more precisely, of historiography) in the modern era belong also the intense controversies over the nature of history and the task of historiography, many precipitated by criticisms (fair and unfair) of Ranke.[30]

Whether history is a science was controversial. Thus J.B. Bury (1861–1927) began and ended his Oxford inaugural lecture declaring that "history is a science, no less and no more" (from Stern, *Varieties of History*, 210, 223). But at Cambridge, G.M. Trevelyan argued that history is scientific in sifting evidence and accumulating facts but is literary and educational in writing the narrative of the past. "Writing is not, therefore, a secondary but one of the primary tasks of the historian" (Stern, 239). J.G. Droysen had seen this in 1868: "History is the only science enjoying the ambiguous fortune of being required to be at the same time an art" (Stern, 139).

Hegel sought to comprehend the nature of history as such, and, emphasizing philosophical idealism, contended that history is the self-actualizing in time of the Absolute/Idea/Spirit/Mind (which Marx's materialist view would turn upside down). Though Hegel's idealist metaphysics was widely abandoned, four of his emphases continue to influence discussions of the nature of history: his contention that the real is rational (i.e., reality can be understood), that history must be understood as a whole, that history does not ground itself but has a transcendent ground, and that history is telic (it has a goal).

By the latter quarter of the nineteenth century, the passion to be "scientific" begat a Weltanschauung called *Historismus* (the usual English approximation is historicism). Though severely criticized, especially in the twentieth century,[31] in 1936 the eminent historian Friedrich Meinecke (1862–1954) hailed historicism as the German contribution second only to the Reformation.[32] No theologian affirmed historicism more vigorously than Ernst Troeltsch (1865–1923).[33] Troeltsch's view is significant for the present discussion because his theoretical understanding of history undergirded what Wrede envisioned and Bousset delivered.

In 1898, like Wrede's summons the year before, Troeltsch called on Protestant theology to accept unreservedly the consequences of "what is signified by the historical method, the historical mode of thought, and the historical sense"—in short, "the effect of modem historical methodology on the interpretation of Christianity itself."[34] Instead of adducing historical information piecemeal to illumine and warrant segments of Christianity, Troeltsch emphasized three aspects of the historical method: (a) ongoing criticism of the sources yields only probable results; (b) "the irrefutably given uniformity and homogeneity of human events" allows no exceptions (miracles); (c) and the interrelatedness of all historical events precludes isolating Christianity's development (a point important for Bousset; see above). The historical method, "once admitted at any one point, necessarily draws every-thing into its train." Indeed, "give the historical method an inch and it will take a mile." Because the historical method's three aspects work in concert, it "relativizes everything."[35] Accepting the method means nothing less than the "historicizing of our entire thinking," thereby "transforming everything and ultimately exploding the very form of earlier theological method" (particularly any appeal to God's mirac-ulous intervention or to authoritative scripture).[36] For Troeltsch, it is obvious that "the historical method necessarily leads to a theology that is based on the history of religion" as he understood it.

The History of Religion

Ironically, though Christianity's power to shape societies in the West declined, religion became more fascinating for intellectuals in academe and beyond, as archeologists provided new evidence about religions in the world of the Bible (and elsewhere). Max Müller at Oxford gener-ated a 50-volume set of *Sacred Books of the East*; James Frazier's *Golden Bough* provided a popularized treatment of ancient religions' mythol-ogies and rites. Even though "religion" itself eluded a definition that was commonly accepted, by the end of the nineteenth century there emerged a new discipline, *Religionswissenschaft* (literally, the science of religion), spawning a new profession as well—*Religionswissenschaftler*, whose first congress met in Stockholm in 1897.[37]

But *Religionswissenschaft* must be distinguished from *Religionsges-chichte* (the history of religion), which refers to a particular approach developed, at the end of the nineteenth century, by a group of young academics at Göttingen, among them Wrede, Bousset, and Troeltsch.[38] Despite differences, they shared a distinct view of the historical task in the study of religion: without relying on metaphysics or the truth claims of Christian doctrine, to grasp what religion is *generically*[39] so that one could explain its particular contingent manifestations *genetically.* Though others labeled the young mavericks *die religionsges-chichtliche Schule* (the history of religion school),[40] Troeltsch insisted that one could not speak of a "school" but only of a method used by those scholars "who had given up the last remnant of a core of super-naturally revealed truths in the Bible, and who work exclusively with the universally valid methods of psychology [essential for understanding the religious a priori] and history."[41]

Their work had three hallmarks: First, in effect accepting Schlei-ermacher's dictum that doctrine is "religious affections set forth in speech," their historical interpretation emphasized the religious experi-ence behind or in religious ideas, institutions, and practices. What a text says *about* the deity expresses an experience *of* the deity. Experienced religion, not doctrine, was to be the real subject matter to be discov-ered, described, and explained historically—that is, comparatively and genetically as Wrede called for, Bousset did, and Troeltsch justified.[42]

Second, in situating the emergence of Christianity in the his-tory of religion, these scholars explored the similarities and differences between Christianity and non-Christian ideas, assumptions, hopes, and practices, usually inferring influences from similarities, thus turn-ing the comparative observation into the genetic construction. While depriving Christianity of its uniqueness offended conservatives, it encouraged liberals by anchoring Christianity in the religiosity shared with all humanity.

Gunkel's interpretation of the "school" began by saying that "from its beginning and . . . in certain essential points, New Testament religion stood under the influence of foreign religions, and . . . this influence reached the men of the New Testament through Judaism" and concluded by asserting, "Christianity is a syncretistic religion."[43] Mediating Judaism had itself become syncretistic, both in its Palestinian form, whose apocalyptic element had absorbed ancient Babylonian and Iranian motifs, and in its hellenized forms. The syncretistic non-Jewish religions that influenced emerging Christianity had been penetrated by "oriental" elements (as Bousset argued in detail). Characteristically, the "school" relied heavily on the research of those classicists, philologists, and other experts in antiquity who were interested in popular religion. Especially important was Bousset's colleague and friend, Richard Reitzenstein (1861–1931), who repeatedly assembled widely scattered evidence to posit a pervasive, syncretistic redemption religion, centered in a heavenly redeemer bearing various names (e.g., Adam, Son of Man), the primal human (the *Urmensch*)—a religion conveying salvation by sacramental participation in the redeemer (i.e., through cultic mysteries).[44]

Third, many in the "school" also saw themselves as Christians with a clear apologetic role: in industrialized and increasingly "secularized" Germany, to resume Schleiermacher's task of vindicating religion as such in order to validate its specifically Christian form. So they described, defended, and advocated their approach in public lectures,[45] and produced the encyclopedia *Religion in Geschichte und Gegenwart* (repeatedly revised),[46] as well as inexpensive paperbacks for the general reader.[47] Bousset was virtually an evangelist for liberal Protestant religion.[48] Troeltsch claimed that comparing the histories of religions will show that Christianity is both the "culmination point" *and* "the convergence point" of all the developed tendencies that can be discovered in religion."[49]

Troeltsch, perceived as the group's systematic theologian, saw theology's task as "grounding the validity of Christianity within the stream of the universal development of the history of religions and over against the entirely analogous claims to validity made by the other great religions," after one has given up "the supernatural revelation of the Bible." He seemed quite confident that history enabled theologians to meet the challenge.

In "constructing out of history a world of ideas that shall be normative for us," Troeltsch saw theology's *first* task to be "establishing, on the basis of a philosophy of the comparative history of religions, the fundamental and universal supremacy of Christianity for our own culture and civilization" (i.e., reasserting Christendom). The *second* is to identity the "essence of Christianity," which he saw as "faith in the rebirth and higher birth of the creature who is alienated from God—a regeneration effected through the knowledge of God in Christ. The consequence of this regeneration is union with God and social fellowship so as to constitute the kingdom of God." The *third* is to expound this essence in the conceptions of God, world, humanity, redemption, eternal life, etc., thereby serving the current needs "growing out of the religious unrest and crisis due to the intellectual and ethical upheaval of our age."[50]

Troeltsch was not disturbed when he exchanged Christianity's absoluteness for its unsurpassed historical development, for he believed that all the modern Christian needs "is the certainty that within the Christian orientation to life there is an authentic revelation of God and that nowhere is a greater revelation to be found. This certainty he can discover even in a purely historical consideration of Christianity."[51]

Clearly, the historical method, though often resisted, repeatedly restricted to annotations, and sometimes accepted only reluctantly, has affected every aspect of Christian belief and all believers as well—because in one way or another, it has penetrated both the minds of moderns and "the modern mind." Indeed, after Christianity's early hellenization, nothing has had a wider, deeper, impact on Western Christianity than "history"—that is, the ethos and effect of critical historiography. Troeltsch saw this and affirmed it. The gains in knowledge of Christianity's origins, and of its embeddedness in kaleidoscopic antiquity, have been enormous. What is not to be overlooked is that its misjudgments are correctible. Nonetheless, its sovereignty was not unambiguous. Indeed, the character of Christianity's identity—the continuity of its determinative content—was at stake in the outcome of historical analyses of its foundational texts, the Gospels, and in the alternative constructions of its origins. That ambiguity must now be examined briefly.

The Hegemony of the Ambiguous

History—as a particular method, a comprehensive perspective, and a way of thinking as well as a range of conclusions about the past—had

come to dominate much biblical study long before Troeltsch defended
its role without appealing to Idealist (Hegelian) metaphysics. Despite
resistance, including "the heresy trials" of William Robertson Smith in
Scotland and Charles Augustus Briggs in America, many Scripture readers found the results of the historical method to be liberating, for it
freed them from the burden of trying to believe the unbelievable.[52] The
positive role of history and of critical historiography in modem religious
life—however that is viewed—should be neither forgotten nor doubted.

Not only were the Bible's miracles set aside, but repeatedly its historical information about events and authors was replaced by alleged
facts. In addition, ideas deemed untenable to modern minds could
now be viewed, whether with condescension or empathy, as the legacy
of the prescientific era. Likewise, after geology and evolution extended
the past by millions of years, it followed that humankind did not "fall"
from an originally pure state but "rose" from a quasi-human stage to
homo sapiens with a continually developing moral consciousness.
Further, those who found "God talk" problematic, if not impossible
altogether, could relax: Since modem historiography does not include
"God" among the actors in human affairs (except as an idea, true or
not, in human actors' minds), they need not read the Bible as the
account of God's efforts to redeem humans; they could (and did) read
and explain it as the epic of the human quest for an intelligibly credible
and morally worthy God.

In various ways, then, for the relatively secure, better-
educated middle and upper middle classes, modern historiography's
Weltanschauung provided a religious counterpart to the Whig interpretation of history: the story of the progress of the morally deserv-
ing toward fulfillment in freedom. The historical approach to religion,
in other words, enabled many persons in the rising middle classes to
retain at least an attenuated link to the inherited Christian religion
without ceasing to be "modern." At the same time, the gains were not
free, for history's sovereign power also brought several problematic
consequences that are still with us.

To begin with, apart from a few notable exceptions like Barth and Bultmann, Christian theology has relied on a view of history that in retrospect was remarkably naive: Since what happened in the past is history, history is what happened in the past. Actually, of course, "history" is always less than what happened and usually more as well—the former because all historiography is selective, the latter because the known past inevitably involves the knowing historian as well. In weighing evidence and "reconstructing" what probably happened and why it did (or did not), the historian's thumb is always on the scale too. Thus, whether the resulting "history" is "less" or "more," it does not, and cannot reproduce the past that happened, the actual past, no matter how much the historian's rhetoric makes the past "come alive." Because a gap between the actual past and the constructed past is inevitable and therefore undeniable, the quest for an uninterpreted history is a search for El Dorado.[53]

"History," then, is the construction by historians who turn critically assessed evidence from the actual past (often accidentally available) into a plausible *portrayal of the probable past* that can corroborate, complete, or correct the *inherited past*. As Hayden White sees it, the historian writes "a verbal structure in the form of a narrative prose that purports to be a model, or icon, of past structures and processes in the interest of *explaining what they were by representing them*."[54] Further, since "no unified social or historical science has provided a fund of theory for historical explanation or guidelines for the selection and organization of historical data" (Iggers, *New Directions*, 11), much of "history" reflects the historian's own context, purpose, stance toward the subject matter, etc.[55] Also, turning evidence from the actual past into "history" inevitably makes the portrayed past more coherent, more understandable than the past that was; especially important is the rhetoric of "explanation."[56] *Still*, the fact that writing "history" is a literary art requiring imagination does not imply that the result is fiction or fantasy.[57]

Given the inherent ambiguity of "history," it is not surprising that the consequences of applying historical criticism to the Bible proved to be ambiguous as well. For one thing, it changed the way the Bible was to be read, thereby making it a different kind of book. The church's canon became an important Reader in ancient Hebrew and early Christian literature put into an historical sequence constructed by critics. Moreover, as Wrede and Troeltsch saw, once it was agreed that *every* part of the Bible—including its antecedent traditions and alleged texts—must be read in its original setting if the past was to be constructed accurately, the Bible became a "source" among sources of information whose reliability was not a given but subject to critical assessment. Now many Christians, instead of interpreting the world through the lens of Scripture, began interpreting the Bible according to scholarship's historical constructions.[58] Some regarded it as the literary deposit of the historical development of true religion, reached in Jesus; others saw it as the record of God's saving acts in history. While both views made "history" central, the former relied on "progress" and the latter on evidence, itself subject to historical evaluation. Despite the undeniable gains in knowledge about the ways the Bible was deeply rooted in the past, expecting so much of ambiguous "history" often stifled serious theological interpretation of writings that are inherently religious.

Ironically, the ambiguity of "history's" hegemony is visible also from a somewhat different angle. Despite the "secularization" of history that followed once historians ceased to regard God as the chief actor, the religious importance of history actually increased.[59] Of the many facets of this development, one merits brief discussion here. Once the divine doer was excluded from scientific explanations of both human and natural history, the gap was filled by another totalizing entity: Troeltsch, after saying, "Give the historical method an inch and it will take a mile," astutely added that history "seems to bear a certain similarity to the devil." Since the devil is the counterpart to God, Troeltsch might have compared history's totalism—its claim to be the comprehensive reality in which we "live and move and have our being"—to God's erstwhile sovereignty, especially important in rigorous Calvinism. In any case, where our culture has become dechristianized, it has become common to regard history as the final judge; it is to *its* verdict that we entrust the meaning of our lives and deeds. So, too, God's providence has become history's progress, and God's kingdom made into history's telos, for whose attainment we strive but for whose arrival we do not wait. History, like God, is both powerful and wise, subduing the unruly and instructing the teachable; it governs events by "laws" discernible by the astute. Even so, History's ways are as inscrutable as the now absent God's.

But nowhere in theology has history's hegemony had a greater impact than in Christology.

Christology within the Limits of History Alone[60]

History's hegemony in the modern era has been exercised primarily in two interacting ways: (a) through criticism (critical assessment of the inherited views of the past and of the relevant evidence) and (b) through construction (its explanatory tools relying on context, antecedents, influences, consequences, etc.). Both ways affected Christian thought profoundly because each drove a wedge between "the Jesus of history" and "the Christ of faith."[61] Although many items in the Gospels were judged "unhistorical," frequently "the Jesus of history" (a.k.a. "the historical Jesus"), constructed according to the canons of modern historiography, was thought to be more credible as well as more relevant than the Christological "Jesus Christ" of traditional faith. What needs discussion here, however, is how constructing the "Jesus of history" has impacted NT Christology.

Often the language generally used has blurred the issues. First, Strauss's contrast between Jesus (history) and Christ (which he called "myth") has had mischievous effects, for "myth" has many meanings. Second, the implications of "the historical Jesus" too have been mischievous because its users commonly thought it referred to the man "as he really was in his own time and place," whereas it actually refers to the historians' Jesus (often a particular historian's Jesus!). Third, also "the Jesus of history," is not the "actual Jesus"; that figure eludes our grasp.

Still, adding "of history" to the personal name is not superfluous, for it has two functions: It distinguishes *this* constructed Jesus from others (e.g., the Jesus of hymnody, or medieval art), and it reminds us that the man was also *of* history, as subject to its character as are other humans. Whereas classic Christology spoke of Jesus's true humanity, which coexisted with his divinity, "the Jesus of history" often assumes only his humanness, leaving his divinity a matter of opinion—that is, optional.

The extent to which "the Jesus of history" is separated from Christology largely depends on who bears the burden of proof (and who assigns it). For conservatives, it is the critic who must show why certain reports about Jesus in the Gospels are not facts; for liberal critics, the Gospels bear the burden of showing why they are reliable. The tension between these views has perpetuated arguments over method and the proper criteria for locating reliable evidence. Those determined to use only what was undoubtedly said by Jesus often relied especially on the criterion of dissimilarity (or "negative criteria"): Only sayings not traceable to Jewish ideas in the minds of the first believers or not contaminated by Christian beliefs are to be accepted as truly from Jesus himself. Inevitably, this criterion isolated Jesus from both his heritage and his legacy. Though recently, critics have relied less on the "negative criteria" and more on the criteria of plausibility, many assumptions of the "negative criteria" live on.

The Gospels (and all oral or written Jesus traditions on which they are probably based) are permeated by Christian convictions about Jesus's identity and significance. They deliberately narrate a *Christological Jesus of history,* who from time to time articulates a Christology and in whom the "supernatural" occasionally appears; for the Evangelists, *that* is the sort of person Jesus "really was," decades before their own time. So the Gospels characteristically weave seamlessly into their accounts diverse materials that are manifestly

Christology-laden: miracle stories, legends, references to the role of the Spirit in Jesus's life, statements that correlate Jesus's deeds with Scripture, and his sayings articulating the religious significance of his mission and impending death. These are the very materials that critical historiography sets aside as "unhistorical" or "inauthentic," deeming them so *in accord with* early Christian beliefs about Jesus that they probably were *produced* by Christians. The critical historian must therefore construct "the Jesus of history" and explain his significance without just this evidence. What are the consequences for a Christology that is based on such a Jesus?

Jesus without Christology

To begin with, given the hegemony of critical historiography, the contrast between the "Jesus of history"[62] and the Jesus of the NT has prompted some to doubt that NT Christology is legitimate. What Hendrikus Boers boldly stated four decades ago is now widely thought, though often unstated: "The view of Jesus in the New Testament was not historically true of Jesus himself. This undercuts the basic assumption on which the Christology of the New Testament depends, namely, that it is an expression of the truth about the historical Jesus."[63] On the other hand, from the same contrast, Robert Morgan drew a quite different conclusion: Where the NT Jesus confronts the historians' Jesus, the NT theologian's first task is "to demolish the historian's claim to possess 'the truth' about Jesus, and so make room for Christological claims which assert a fuller and obligatory truth about Jesus, not simply an optional preference of believers."[64]

The demolition that Morgan called for is aimed not at the historians' constructions but at their unalloyed confidence in them, evident in Boers's assertion. Particularly significant is the assumption that NT Christology is legitimate when it coincides with what was "historically true of Jesus himself" (primarily his own self-interpretation but also the "facts" about his life). The fruit of this assumption is the two-sided *distortion of the discipline* of NT Christology. On the one hand, the inevitable ongoing debates over "the truth about the historical Jesus" nourish the misunderstanding that Christological questions and historical questions are virtually identical, thereby abetting the transformation of NT Christology into history. On the other hand, it supports the misunderstanding that NT Christology is valid when it repeats, expounds, or elaborates Jesus's own self-interpretation insofar as it is knowable within the limits of history alone. Both forget that the task is to explain the Christian understandings of Jesus's religious significance that jelled after Easter (thus Morgan's "obligatory truth about Jesus"). A week after Easter, whoever understood Jesus's significance the same way as a week before Palm Sunday did not believe that God raised him from the dead. (The story of "doubting Thomas" in John 20 makes this very point.) That is, believing that God raised Jesus from the dead changes the kind of continuity between the pre-Easter Jesus and the post-Easter Jesus Christ that characterizes NT Christology. Whatever problems moderns themselves may have with Jesus's resurrection, the discipline of *NT* Christology cannot act as if Easter did not occur. (For the role of the resurrection in NT Christology, see chapter 2.)

Further, compared with classic Christology, within the limits of history alone the *content* of Christology becomes constricted because the norms of historiography limit what can be said about the relation between God and Jesus. Concretely, history-restricted Christology can speak only of Jesus's own religious relation to God, whereas classic Christology, based on the supernatural-charged Jesus of the Gospels, claims that God was an active participant in Jesus himself, not only the key factor in motivating and sustaining his mission. The doctrine of Christ's two natures later grounded this conviction metaphysically, and thereby accounted for the miraculous in Jesus's mission and differentiated his very being from everyone else's. But once modern historiography excluded the supernatural-laden materials as unhistorical, Christology based squarely and solely on rescuing the "Jesus of history" inevitably replaced God's involvement in Jesus with Jesus's devotion to God. Within the limits of history alone, God was not the *intrinsic* actor in the Jesus event, but the point of reference *extrinsic* to Jesus, the reality to which he looked until the end of his life. While the cross now discloses the character and extent of *his* commitment to God, it does not reveal *God's* commitment to us. This Jesus invites us to identify with him; in him, God does not identify with us. In short, within the limits of critical history alone, the "Jesus of history" becomes the first Christian saint, a heroic figure whose teachings instruct us *about* God and whose fidelity *to* God becomes salvific when it becomes contagious.

The fountainhead of this kind of Christology was Schleiermacher who construed Christ's divinity as Jesus's unbroken God-consciousness. Later, liberal Protestantism emphasized the religious experience of Jesus, which, by being prototypical, transforms our own relation to God, thereby preserving some of the significance of Jesus as redeemer. Those Christians who welcomed biblical criticism also welcomed this way of understanding the religious significance of Jesus, for such Christology, centered in the "Jesus of history," was disentangled from offensive doctrines of salvation and linked instead to the modern view that religion must be inspiring.

That such Christology, being unable to undergird classical Christianity, supports a revisionist Christianity is clear. Not so clear is whether or how a Christianity with such a Christology (i.e., without a participating God at its core) can have a redemptive word for a death-bound humanity that often is also simultaneously guilt-ridden and guilt-denying. From the standpoint of both classic Christology and the NT, at any rate, one must ask whether a Christology that emphasizes Jesus's piety is a genuine Christology at all, or a form of hero-worship, a *Jesuology*.

The significance of Jesus, of course, is neither limited to religion nor articulated only by Christians using theological language. Indeed, within the limits of history alone, the significance of Jesus often is implied in how he is depicted, as well as in how his positive impact in human affairs is assessed. While in such cases the religious significance is usually unstated, the result is nonetheless a virtual Christology because it functions like a real Christology.

Surrogate Christology in the Guise of History[65]

The situation is ironic: Despite the long effort to describe and explain Jesus himself by separating him from Christology, the resulting "Jesus of history" is not Christology-free, for reasons already stated. To them must be added another factor: the historian's judgments. Within the limits of history alone, the historian often must do what Christology does, inasmuch as constructing the "Jesus of history" shifts questions about Jesus's significance to the historian who conveys (implicitly or explicitly) a view of Jesus's import—in effect, a "Christology." The result, because unintended, is not a matter of deception.[66]

Bousset's construal of Jesus's religious significance provides a useful example of Christology in the guise of history. Important in NT Christology is Jesus's relation to Israel's sacred text (Scripture) and sacred space (temple). The Gospels use the "prophecy and fulfillment" theme to express their views of Jesus's relation to the Bible and to Judaism. Historical criticism, however, disallowed the theme as an explanation of Jesus but expanded the picture of Jesus's interaction with first-century Jewish religion. Thus Bousset, in accord with the perspective of the "history of religion school," said that Jesus *completed* the historical trend in the history of religion by purifying his people's religion.

Building on his magisterial *Die Religion des Judentums* (1903), where he argued that Palestinian Judaism never fully overcame its particularisms, his *Jesus* (1907) claimed that the trend toward inwardness (essential for universalism) reached its high point in Jesus: "the entire sacred cult of his country contributed nothing to the core of his piety"—a view repeated in his *What Is Religion?* Bousset's Jesus was "the noblest and most perfect [figure] that has been granted to humanity on its long journey from the lower stage to the higher." So he is "the Captain who guides everyone to God . . . we *see* . . . in his personality the presence of God, and so we gladly confess that God was in Christ"—not metaphysically, but functionally for our perceptive value judgment tells us so.[67]

More important here than correcting Bousset's history and taming Smith's exuberance (in note 68) is noting what such construals of Jesus's religious significance imply when seen theologically. Anticipating chapter 2, Christology does more than praise Jesus with a special vocabulary; it also claims that who he was and what he did deals decisively with the human condition, however, that is diagnosed. Seen from the standpoint of the NT, then, the basic question to be asked of any surrogate Christology functioning in portrayals of the Jesus of history is: *How deeply does it actually reach into the human condition?* Closely related: *What reason is there to think that he can transform it?* From a yet different angle: *Do not such unintended Christologies imply that the traditional views of Jesus's religious significance have been obviated by our progress?* Indeed, is Jesus himself, though honored as an exemplary figure, no longer necessary for human flourishing? Some, in fact, have doubted that he ever was.

Christology without Jesus

Whereas those who championed a Jesus without Christology believed they were liberating a vital, modern Christianity from bondage to no-longer-tenable doctrines, those who advocated a Christology without Jesus were convinced that they were emancipating the real, abiding truth of religion from Christianity's unwarranted preoccupation with a specific person in a particular history.

At the end of the eighteenth century, Immanuel Kant's *Religion Within the Limits of Reason Alone* argued that the idea of "humanity well pleasing to God," for which we are obligated to strive, does not require embodiment in a single, particular individual, for the idea is given with the in-built sense of obligation itself. Neither the truth nor the power of this idea depends on Jesus having actualized it himself. "This idea as an archetype is already present in our reason."

Having asserted that since "we ought to conform" to this idea, we "must be able to do it," he also claimed that "the presence of this archetype in the human soul is in itself sufficiently incomprehensible without . . . the assumption that it is hypostasized to a particular individual" (55–57).

A few decades later, David Friedrich Strauss came to a similar conclusion, though by following Hegel instead of Kant. Strauss affirmed the incarnation as the unification of the divine and the human but insisted that it never happened in a single person—an impossibility, he thought—but it is in fact occurring in humanity as a whole (without completing what had begun in Jesus). Hegel's influence is clear when he declared, "Humanity is the union of the two natures—God became man, the infinite manifesting itself in the finite, the finite spirit remembering its infinitude." Implying that he is interpreting, not replacing, Christian theology, he said, "It is Humanity that dies, rises, and ascends the heaven, for from the negation of its phenomenal life ever proceeds a higher spiritual life. By faith in this Christ . . . man is justified before God." This Christ is "the infinitely repeated pulsation of the divine life." The Jesus event "is but a more sensible image of this unending process," he claimed at the end of his *Life of Jesus.*

Strauss did not deny or doubt that there had been a Jesus of Nazareth, but others soon did. Understandably so. "The Christ of Faith" having been separated from "the Jesus of history," for whom historical facts became scarcer, while the similarities between the former and ancient myths of redeemers seemed to accumulate, it was not difficult to infer that "the Christ of faith" created "the Jesus of history." So reasoned Bruno Bauer (1809–1882), erstwhile Hegelian, and a few others. Today, most scholars believe that Jesus had once lived and was crucified on Pilate's orders, while many also suspect that much Christology, being older than Jesus, was applied to him, as Bousset argued.

Whatever one's views of that likelihood, through the centuries only a Christology that is centered in Jesus and inseparable from him, has persuaded the minds, energized the devotion, and stimulated the imagination of believers. Is it likely that the nature of Christology itself largely accounts for this?

Meanwhile, as this discussion moves forward, it is useful to take along one thing that chapter 1 has shown: Making NT Christology a theological discipline that is historically informed requires learning not only about the circumstances that influenced what the NT says about Jesus Christ; it entails also coming to terms with the way our own histories shape the way we understand what Christology is and does, visible already in the NT.

﹋ 2 ﹌

THE SUBJECT REDEFINED

It really takes a great deal of theology to revolutionize theology.
—P.T. Forsyth

What we need to do is to return the river to its bed.
—Paul Ricoeur

REDEFINING NEW TESTAMENT Christology requires a grasp of Christology as such, of what any Christology does and why it does it at all. Such an understanding is generic, not genetic (as Wrede's program). Outlining what a generic approach entails is therefore this chapter's initial assignment. Its second task is to note some of ways the NT speaks of Jesus Christ (thus responding to Wrede's claim that the NT writings do not really permit talk of their Christology). The chapter's third purpose is to redefine NT Christology as an historically informed theological discourse.

Understanding Christology Generically

The sheer diversity of Christologies evokes the questions *Just what is Christology? What is it really about? More important, what is it talking about?*

Generic and Genetic Understanding

The distinction is significant, for it was the genetic understanding, championed by Wrede, followed by Bousset, and explained theoretically by Troeltsch that made it possible to turn NT Christology into the history of early Christology. Both approaches concern the religious significance of Jesus, but they ask different questions in order to provide different kinds of explanations.

The *genetic* inquiry—the core of historiography—being interested in developments that matter seeks to account for what followed from certain events (themselves contingent on what preceded them), how those consequences came about, and which of them became turning points in retrospect. Essential for such a historical purpose is ascertaining the correct sequence of events and sources of information about them. Essential for a *generic* understanding of Christology, on the other hand, is ascertaining the logical sequence of thoughts and their coherence. Important as it is to distinguish the genetic from the generic study of Christology so that each can ask its own questions, the two modes of understanding do not exclude each other categorically, for just as the genetic is theologically informed, so the generic is historically informed. Nevertheless, it is one thing to ask, "What follows in time and space from a particular configuration of events and persons?" but another to ask, "What logic or kind of reasoning configures a specific set of ideas, images, sorts of actions, as well as assumptions, into a coherent, intelligible statement of Jesus's religious significance?"

A generic understanding, like a genetic inquiry, distinguishes Christology's formal structure from its material content (its various particular images and ideas, e.g., savior, purification, bread). The (more stable) formal element orders the diverse material elements into a coherent intelligible whole, the way syntax turns a string of words, each understandable by itself, into a sentence that makes sense. A Christological sentence or paragraph makes sense when it explains the significance Christians find in Jesus Christ. Put as an epigram, the salvation wrought by/in/through Jesus makes Christology necessary; in turn, Christology explains how this salvation is possible.

For nearly two millennia, Christians have expressed this significance in ever-various ways: visually in art and architecture; kinetically in dance and liturgical acts; audibly in music; and verbally in confession ("Jesus is Lord." 1 Corinthians 12:3, or "Jesus is cool!" or "Thank you, Jesus!"). Such verbal expressions are Christological but are not Christology proper because they express; they do not explain or justify the assertion. Christology requires a logos, as the word Christology implies: the rationale that warrants calling Jesus [the] "Christ," the expected redeemer of God's people. (So firmly did this earliest interpretation of Jesus's religious significance establish itself that within two decades Paul used "Christ" as a proper name.)

A generic understanding of Christology is also systemic. Just as a genetic understanding sees developments as part of larger wholes, so a generic view sees how Christology functions within a more comprehensive view of reality. Systemic understanding entails more than grasping discrete ideas about Jesus, or even an aggregate of them; it requires ascertaining how and why the various ideas and assumptions "work" together. It is therefore alert to the way changes in one part ripple through the whole—like the way delays at one airline's hub changes flight plans throughout the system.

When understood generically and viewed systemically, a fully stated Christology leaves no aspect of Christian thought untouched. What matters here, however, is understanding how Christology achieves its purpose, how it "works."

Christology's Correlates

Understanding how Christology "works" as well as what it says requires using an instrument that is appropriate for the task: Explaining why and how Jesus Christ's impact on *our* relation to God is grounded in *his* relation to God. Christology is never only about Jesus Christ; it is always about these dual relationships, for they account for his religious significance. In this book, these twin relationships are called Christology's correlates.

The *theological* correlate anchors Christ's ability to redeem in his relation to God/in God's relation to him. The *anthropological/*

soteriological correlate is twofold because the soteriological cure must fit the anthropological disease. Moreover, the theological and anthropological/soteriological correlates imply each other. To grasp their conjunction is to understand how Christology pursues its purpose.

Also, since the cure fits the condition, both must be of the same order, share the same conceptual field; otherwise, a given Christological statement will make no sense. Thus, a moral plight calls for a moral resolution, an inherently metaphysical condition, like finitude, needs a metaphysical transformation, not a moral transaction like forgiveness. Similarly, the cure for ignorance is knowledge, not pardon (unless the ignorance is self-willed).

It is this reciprocity between anthropology and soteriology that allows one to reason from either plight to solution or from solution to plight. For those who begin with the human plight, Christology explains why Christ is the solution; for others, the solution in Christ discloses the real problem, not visible before—the way a builder's plumb line reveals a wall's unnoticed slant. The difference between these approaches is less important for grasping the Christological assertion's content than it is for surmising how a theologian arrived at his conclusion—as will be evident in the discussion of Paul's theology.

The logical relation between condition and cure becomes explicitly Christological as soon as one asks how Jesus did or did not participate in the debilitating condition. In classical Christology, a figure essentially undifferentiated from other humans cannot affect or mediate their redemption, because he himself instantiates the problem; only a figure who differs from us precisely in what distorts our relation to God and neighbor can change us where it really matters. He must differ enough to change us, be enough like us to reach us; neither angels nor androids can do this. The ancient arguments over the nature and extent of Jesus's humanness were struggles to establish conceptually the reality of the salvation promised by the gospel and experienced by those who believed it.

Whereas the anthropological/soteriological correlate relates Jesus to human sin and salvation, the theological correlate accounts for his capacity to save by the way it links him to God. Moreover, since the nature of the human condition determines the nature of salvation, the theological correlate shows why the worse the view of the human condition the greater capacity to save becomes; otherwise, some conditions would be beyond his reach. In short, the deeper the dilemma, the "higher" the Christology. Accordingly, classical Christology has insisted that neither an exemplary human being nor a supernatural creature can actually convey a metaphysical salvation that transforms a metaphysical state. Only the uncreated, noncontingent Creator can change the creature's nature or being, transform the temporal into the eternal, the mortal into the immortal. By the same reasoning, if the heart of humanity's plight is not a debilitating metaphysical condition, a "lower" Christology will suffice. An optimistic reading of humanity's situation regularly generates a Christology in which the Creator God does not, and need not, participate directly in the savior's being but instead can be the reality that motivates and shapes Jesus's word and way. Then Jesus need not differ from us metaphysically (by having two "natures"); it is enough that he differs from us morally, in his repeatable attainment. Nor need his religious significance include a final metaphysical transformation at the border of phenomenal existence, for heeding his word and following his way heals our moral atrophy and energizes our will to achieve whatever measure of the good is presently possible within this world.

The more fully one grasps how Christology "works," how its correlates function, the more apparent is its audaciousness. Lest this audacity be too easily regarded as an expression of Christian arrogance or as a by-product of early Christian enthusiasm, it needs to be understood and acknowledged.

Christology's Audacity

The audacity of Christology should not be overlooked or taken for granted. Even if one holds that Jesus's salvific impact on the human condition is remarkable but is neither decisive nor adequate for everyone, it is Christology's task to explain how also this lesser impact is grounded precisely in Jesus Christ. And the more the anthropological/ soteriological correlate shows why this salvation has neither temporal, nor geographical, nor ethnic, nor cultural, nor socioeconomic boundaries but is available to all persons and peoples, the more audacious it becomes to insist that redemption is inseparable from a person who lived within the bounds of a particular society, people, place, and time. Put somewhat differently: The Christian religion's insistence that precisely the first-century Jesus of Nazareth is the irreplaceable redeemer makes Christology audacious—and keeps it so.

Indeed, so inseparable is the individual man Jesus from his religious significance that our earliest records (Paul's letters) either add that significance to his personal name or substitute "Christ" for his name altogether. It should not surprise us, then, to find that Christology regularly assumes, and sometimes asserts, that Jesus Christ will not be supplemented or surpassed, however much his religious significance may be elaborated, and expanded, or otherwise celebrated.

Moreover, even though the Christ-wrought salvation is actualized only partly and often inconsistently, Christology remains audacious because it is a particular form of "faith seeking understanding," not the reverse. While Christology is often appropriated by efforts to persuade someone to become a believer, its defining task is to explain what for believers is a given: that the Christ-wrought salvation is real and really true, even if it is experienced now as a down payment, as an oft-beclouded dawn, as a pledge of an uncompromised future freedom. Indeed, one might well say that Christology explains redemption's "already" and copes with its "not yet."

Encountering Christology in the New Testament

It is quite likely that even a casual browser will soon discover that not one of the NT's 27 writings consists only of Christology. One will discover instead that the NT's Christology is embedded in a collection of early Christian texts produced mostly to edify, less to explain, and not at all to entertain. As Wrede noted, here Christology is persistently "practical," showing up regularly to warrant something else—be it an exhortation or a warning, an assurance or a way of life, to name but a few examples. Consequently, the more seriously one takes the pragmatic function of Christology in the NT, the more significant become two aspects of the way Christology manifests itself there: (a) the incompleteness of what is said and (b) the conceptual models that give a visualizable "shape" to the Christ event.

Fragments and Silences

To begin with, to a large extent, it is the practical function of the NT's Christology that explains its incomplete and often fragmentary character: The writers said what they deemed germane for the purpose and left the rest unsaid. They were, after all, Christians writing to and for Christians. In any case, one cannot equate the Christology of a given writing with the Christology of the writer, for their entire Christology is no more visible than an entire iceberg. As we will see in chapter 4, this is as true of Paul, who wrote many letters, as it is of the person who wrote only I Peter or Mark. This first observation is basic for the redefinition of NT Christology.

In addition, Christological incompleteness marks also those passages that may not have been created by the writer but probably were quoted by him, such as the hymnic pieces in John 1:1–14; Philippians 2:5–11; Colossians 1:15–20; and 2 Timothy 3:16. Hymnic passages celebrate the assertions they emphasize. But in being quoted, the function of their inherent Christology can be modified, while its conceptual content is unchanged.

Some passages appear as slices of an actual large piece, thus Ephesians 5:14, in supporting an exhortation to live by the light of Christ, quotes these lines:

> *Sleeper, awake!*
> *Rise from the dead*
> *And Christ will shine on you*

Philippians 4:5 inserts "the Lord is near" into a series of admonitions. In 1 Corinthians 16:20, one word expresses (and compresses) virtually a whole Christology, the exclamatory *Maranatha* (our Lord, Come!). The phrase "the day of our Lord Jesus Christ" (1 Corinthians 1:18) alludes to the same complex of ideas. Also, the more fully stated 1 Thessalonians 1:10 points to a much larger tissue of beliefs: "Wait for his [God's] Son from heaven, whom he raised from the dead—Jesus, who rescues us from the wrath that is coming." Not to be overlooked are pregnant phrases that signal Christ's significance without specifying what it is, such as "through our Lord Jesus Christ," as well as "in Christ" and "for the sake of" (for the benefit of) in 2 Corinthians 5:21: "For our sake [God] made him to be sin who knew no sin, so that in him we might become the righteousness of God."

Especially noteworthy is what the NT does not say about Jesus—concretely, how he is not portrayed or explained in the Gospels' narratives, on the one hand, and what is absent from the explicit Christological interpretations in the Epistles, on the other hand. While the issues that the Epistles addressed may account for what they do not say about Jesus, the silences of the Gospels may have a different kind of explanation. In any case, NT scholarship, for understandable reasons, has concentrated so intently on what the Gospels say Jesus did and said that it often ignored what is absent from the Gospels' portrayals and plots, absences that affect the Christologies built into their narratives. Not germane here is silence about certain personal matters, like whether Jesus was (or had been) married, what he thought of the Essene community at the Dead Sea, or how much Greek he picked up. Pertinent, rather, is absent information that would explain reported events and make the Christological portrayals of Jesus more understandable, at least to modern sensibilities: the origins of his sense of vocation, the motives behind significant turning points in his life, and the character of his inner life.

In all four Gospels, Jesus speaks clearly, albeit in various ways, about his vocation, but in none of them does he or the narrator account for its origins or possible development by providing biographical information, although the Gospels report occasions when he (or the narrator) might have done so.

Mark 6:1 reports Jesus's former neighbors' amazement at his teaching, "Where did this man get all this?" Jesus's response does not answer the question but intensified it: Prophets are honored everywhere except at home. In fact, the Synoptic Gospels imply what Jesus's opponents in John also imply: he was an autodidact (John 7:15). In Luke, already the 12-year-old is the untaught teacher of teachers (2:41–50), but the Evangelist's comment about the youngster's growth (verse 40) does not account for his precociousness. So, too, Jesus's astounding claim, "All things have been delivered to me by my Father," etc. (Matthew 11:27), remains as unexplained as his assertion in John 7:16 that his teaching is really God's. Nor does Jesus explain why the Son of Man *must* suffer, or how he came to this conclusion, or apply it to himself though he does explain why Peter objects to this destiny (Mark 8:31–33).

To the extent that Gospels do account for Jesus's sense of mission and its salient aspects, they rely on divine action (what he saw and heard at his baptism), not on causal or developmental considerations, as moderns view them.

Nor do the Gospels say a word about the motivations behind the turning points in Jesus's mission. Readers can only surmise why he went to John for baptism (Matthew 3:15 is not about motives but result), or why John's arrest prompted Jesus to begin his own, somewhat divergent, mission (Mark 1:14). Also left unsaid are the reasons why he waited until he was near Caesarea Philippi before asking his disciples about his public "image" and making them declare who *they* think he is (Mark 8:27–30). Nor do the Gospels explain why Jesus insisted that his messianic identity, as well as some of his wondrous deeds (Matthew 16:20; Mark 8:4; contrast Mark 5:19) be kept secret, nor do they show any interest in Jesus's motives for making secret arrangements for his arrival in Jerusalem (Mark 14:13–16).

But what the Gospels leave unsaid has been supplied amply by historical critics who at times may even have been right. Be that as it may, the Evangelists evidently assumed that their Christology-permeated portrayals of Jesus would be understood, and could be affirmed as well, without explaining Jesus's motives. Today, a sound grasp of NT Christology should not take for granted what they did not say.

Significant also is the absence of interest in Jesus's private self, the development of his "spiritual life," or his matured "religious experience." Apart from his agony in Gethsemane (absent from John), the Gospels neither say nor imply that he experienced "the dark night of the soul"; the three "temptations" (only in Matthew and Luke) do not describe an inner torment but report his victory over Satan (as in Mark as well). Only in Luke 10:18 does Jesus say he had seen Satan fall like lightning, but not a word more is said about this charismatic event. What Jesus says in John 16:3 could be the headline over the synoptic narratives as well: "Be of good cheer, I have overcome the world." Except for the cry of dereliction (only in Matthew 27:46 and Mark: 15:34), Jesus's relation to God is apparently trouble-free, constant, and exceptionally intimate—but generally not accounted for, described, or explicitly commended as a model. For the Gospels, "the religion of Jesus" is not the gospel, as it was for liberal Christians (see chapter 1, note 67).

So, too, the synoptics are silent about how Jesus "felt" when hearing what the baptismal voice said to him (Mark 1:11) or about him (Matthew 3:17), later repeated to the disciples at the Transfiguration (Mark 9:7). Only Luke 3:21 reports that the newly baptized Jesus was praying when the Spirit came to him, but the prayer's content is not mentioned, as is true also at Luke 11:1, where his praying once prompted the disciples to ask him to teach them how to pray as John had taught his followers. Nor does Luke say that he taught them his own prayer. His prayer in John 17, though addressed to God, really reminds the reader about the nature and significance of Jesus's mission as a whole.

In a word, the occasional, scattered glimpses of Jesus's inner life are few, and have no noticeable influence on the course of events in the Gospel accounts, except for his observance of Passover. That is, they show him to be a real, practicing Jew, but they do not account for the kind of Jew they portray him to have been or for his religious significance. The Christology of the Gospels does not need such information.

Remarkably, while all four Gospels report what Jesus had said about himself and his mission (including the meaning of his impending death), the Epistles repeatedly express the significance of his death and resurrection but never mention what he had said about either one—the sole exception being the liturgically shaped Lord's Supper account (1 Corinthians 11:23–26). The old tradition quoted in 1 Corinthians 15 says that "Christ died for our sins in accord with the Scriptures," not in accord with what he himself had foreseen or said. Moreover, since the Epistles do not quote Jesus even in support of what they emphasize about him, it is not remarkable that they are silent also about his parents, baptism, healings, exorcisms, or proclamation of the kingdom of God. Noteworthy, however, is the fact that the one Christological title that all four Gospels say Jesus used to interpret his death—Son of Man—is completely absent from the Epistles, as is any reference to the role that Jesus tacitly did see himself embodying—prophet and wisdom.

Critics have not hesitated to provide historical explanations for the Epistles' silences, beginning with the observation that Paul wrote all his letters before any of the four Gospels appeared. But the picture becomes more complicated as soon as one remembers that Jesus traditions were circulating during the Apostle's lifetime and that the earliest Gospel (Mark) had been written (as were the alleged antecedents of John) by the time the secondary Pauline Epistles (esp. Colossians, Ephesians, and 2 Thessalonians) were being written and circulated. Further, apart from the intriguing passage in 1 John 5:6, the Johannine Epistles do not *quote* the Johannine Gospel's Jesus, even when they seem to refer to his words. In short, if those critics are right who say the

Gospels' reports of Jesus's self-interpretations do not go back to Jesus himself but were created, not merely formulated, by Christians, why do the Epistles not refer to these words?

One could easily consider other areas where NT Christology is silent, but enough has been noted to reflect on the phenomenon itself. Important is the language used to talk about it. Just as it is important not to convert a writing's silence into evidence of the writer's ignorance or indifference, so it is important not to regard what is *not* said as an "omission," whether accidental or deliberate. Since it is highly doubtful that any NT writer thought *he* left out something significant, "omission" is *our* word for what we find missing—that is, for what we expect to find there. It reflects our disappointment and our judgment. In short, what this brief discussion of "silences" discloses is not flaws in the NT's Christology but the difference between what the writers of the NT thought sufficed to make their Christologies credible and effective and what many moderns assume ought to at least be included if the same aim is to be achieved. In a theological understanding of NT Christology, this difference is to be understood and respected, as the next topic demonstrates.

The Framed Event

In addition to the silences that underscore the incompleteness of what *is* said in NT Christology, one repeatedly finds that the religious significance of Jesus depends on the *theological* context into which references to him are woven. In itself that is unsurprising: A religious significance requires a theological context. Noteworthy, however, is the character of that theological context and its impact: The significance of the Jesus event depends on two realities beyond it, realities that no one saw or could have seen: Jesus's resurrection from the realm of the dead and the preexistence of Christ. (In Matthew and Luke, the virgin birth has a similar function as preexistence; Mark has neither—perhaps the most pregnant silence of all.) At this point, it suffices to clarify the NT meaning of both resurrection and preexistence before examining their appearance in Christologies discussed in Part 2. This sketch should also underline the difference between a theological and a historical context of Jesus's religious significance.

To understand the role of Jesus's resurrection in NT Christology, one must resolutely concentrate on what those who first spoke of it thought *they* were talking about and leave aside all attempts to explain "what really happened" on Easter. Although their writings neither defined "resurrection" per se nor described *Jesus's* resurrection in particular,[1] a number of considerations clearly show what they were *not* talking about: the reanimated or resuscitated corpse, a dead person's restoration to status quo ante (like Lazarus in John 11).

So important is the distinction between resurrection and resuscitation that one would not exaggerate in saying, "Whoever thinks that resurrection resuscitated Jesus's corpse does not, and cannot, understand the New Testament." A resuscitation/reanimation would indeed be a "miracle," an exception to the rules, but it would have little theological significance, however great its religious meaning for the revived person. On believing that a person had come back to life, one might well be amazed and even change one's thinking about life and death but would not find oneself transformed in a world where many things begin to look different. In short, one can believe that a miracle occurred and not be changed, but one cannot believe resurrection occurred and remain the same. "Resurrection," as the NT views it, is that kind of event. In the jargon of theological scholarship, "resurrection," by definition is an *eschatological event.* Jesus's resurrection, therefore, certifies that he is an eschatological event as well. A mere resuscitation cannot have this significance. Nor can the likelihood that Jesus saw himself as an eschatological figure, as the harbinger of God's reign, have this meaning, for his self-interpretation is decisive primarily for those who already believe in him. It does not generate Christian faith.

The abstract formulation "eschatological event" also needs to be understood if one is to grasp what the NT has in view when it refers to Jesus's resurrection.

An eschatological event is an occurrence at the end (*eschaton*) of "this age" and the beginning of "the age to come," when marred historical existence will be transformed into what it ought to be. Described in various ways, in this understanding of human existence, the reality we know and cope with, does not grow into its perfect goal but must be transformed by God's action; of this transformation, resurrection from death into another mode of being is a dramatic instantiation.

Moreover, the expected resurrection was always understood to affect groups, whether all the dead (so they could appear in God's court) or only the righteous (as their reward); never was the resurrection of one person envisaged. Yet this is precisely what the NT asserts. Consequently, the reported resurrection of only Jesus implies either that the report is wrong or that his resurrection is the harbinger of the general resurrection to follow. His resurrection and the general resurrection are separated in time but not in character.[2] The resurrection of precisely and only Jesus validated *him* as the event that inaugurated the New Age, and so confirms his own self-interpretation.

Further, since eschatological events are acts of God, it follows that the NT consistently, with but rare exceptions, says *God* resurrected Jesus. Finally, those who believed that God had done this dared to begin living out of the nonapparent future into the present: Despite history's "not yet," they began being morally transformed by the "already" of Jesus's resurrection.

Whereas resurrection established the significance of Jesus for salvation, the preexistence of Christ guaranteed the significance of his identity. "Preexistence," like "eschatological event," is not part of the NT's vocabulary, but a convenient term for what most of the NT assumes: that Jesus is the embodied, human, historical form of a reality that "was" before there was Jesus.[3] If some moderns regard Jesus's resurrection as a miracle that never happened, others view "the preexistence of Christ" as an oxymoron, like a square circle. How can something "be" before it exists? And what is the point of saying this about Jesus? Before responding to the questions, it is essential to bear in mind that preexistence and incarnation imply each other, and so are logically inseparable yet distinguishable.

Accordingly, the logic of incarnation is discussed at the appropriate places in Part 2. Here the focus is on preexistence per se, its logic, not the concept's origins.

To begin with, to hold that something preexists, that it "is" before it "became," requires one to posit two modes of reality, the one being the empirical, temporal, contingent, ordinary day-to-day world in which beings exist as tangible phenomena; the other, however, is the nonempirical, nontemporal, noncontingent, invisible domain in which entities and beings simply "are" and for which "exist" is inappropriate because what exists is affected by time. Both modes of reality are real, but the nonphenomenal is "really real"; it is absolute, not qualified; it is eternal, not subject to change and finally death. Accordingly, in the NT only the redeemer preexists, never the souls of the redeemed.

Logically, incarnation requires preexistence because something or someone had to "be" before it became a phenomenon (roughly analogous to way an idea or image "is" in the mind before technology or sculpture makes it a tangible object). The NT uses various words to speak of both the preexistent reality (e.g., Son, Christ, Word) and of the transition from preexistence to existence (e.g., became, appeared), without ever describing the transition itself (as some second- and third-century gnostics will do). No New Testament writer combines Jesus's virgin birth with the incarnation or says that that Jesus preexisted. Rather, Jesus is who the preexistent one became.

Significantly, the NT writings show no interest in describing what the preexistent one does/did before becoming Jesus. The one action that is asserted is the preexistent one's role as God's means of creation—and precisely this is not described. This silence implies that while preexistence makes a tacit metaphysical claim, its real concern is soteriological: The Savior redeems what he has made. This soteriological concern will become even more evident when patristic theologians struggle to find the right way to understand the preexistent Son's relation to the heavenly Father.[4]

The Redefinition

Redefining NT Christology as an historically informed theological discourse takes seriously both the adjectival function of "New Testament" and the character of the noun "Christology"; it also invites comments on being "historically informed."

New Testament Christology is the Christology of the New Testament writings. Full stop.

Though this description seems self-evident, its implications are transformative, for they shift the focus from the writers to the writings themselves—that is, to writings that actually exist.

This shift accords with the well-known observation that the act of writing gives the resultant text a significant measure of autonomy vis-à-vis its creator, even if his identity is known. Apart from clues built into the text, the absent writer loses control over its interpretation. Only to a limited extent can scholars retrieve his control by finding traces of his identity, intent, and outlook that may be borne unwittingly by his text. In any case, the shift liberates the study of NT Christology from being unnecessarily embroiled in endless arguments over insoluble problems of the NT's alleged authorship. The search for the author's identity is nonetheless a valid historical quest, even if the NT itself often frustrates the search by deliberately concealing the author.

Of its 27 writings, the author is known only for seven of the 13 letters claiming to be from Paul plus the Book of Revelation (though no one knows who its "John" was); nine others are either anonymous (though having authors assigned to them by unverifiable traditions), or are often said to be pseudonymous. Whatever the verdict in individual cases, an anonymous text deliberately makes its writer's identity irrelevant so that the reader can have direct contact with its content. A pseudonymous text substitutes an alleged author for the real writer who remains anonymous as well. The ambiguities of the evidence of John's authorship will be noted in chapter 5.

The description of New Testament Christology as the Christology of its writing also implies that whatever texts or traditions the Evangelist may have used to compose his Gospel are relevant only as contributions to the resultant Christology of the whole Gospel. Moreover, the Christology detected in writings that no longer exist independently, even if they were recovered, is not a discrete Christology alongside that of a still-existing text used in Matthew and Luke, namely Mark. Recovering as best one can the Christologies of no longer existent texts (e.g., Q) is important for the history of Christology, but New Testament Christology is the Christology of texts that still exist.

Redefining New Testament Christology as a historically informed theological discourse makes the renewal of New Testament Christology possible; indeed, renewing it requires redefinition. Redefinition is not restoration, which looks to the past. Renewal looks to the future. Without renewal, the history of early Christian Christology also grows sterile.

Part 2

ONE JESUS, FOUR CHRISTOLOGIES

❧ **3** ❧

MATTHEW

Jesus and Our Rectitude

The more narrowly Matthew's purposes are defined, the less compelling are the explanations.

—Graham N. Stanton

Christian theology is the theology not of illumination but of conversion.

—P.T. Forsyth

JESUS'S WORDS IN the Sermon on the Mount alert us to the concern of Matthew's Christology: "Unless your righteousness exceeds that of the scribes and Pharisees, you will never enter the kingdom of heaven" (5:20). That stern warning elicits disturbing questions. Why is precisely *their* righteousness inadequate? Were they not the very ones known for their deep commitment to doing God's will, stated in the written law and detailed in the oral tradition of its requirements? So how does the required righteousness differ from theirs? And how does Jesus know that? More important, how is Jesus himself related to what he requires of others? To answer such questions, it is essential to read Matthew in a way that allows its Christology to become visible.

On Reading Matthew

Matthew was not written for a curious public but for a church (*ekklēsia*, assembly); the initial *readers'* circumstances affected both the way Matthew was *constructed* and the *portrait* of Jesus that the narrative creates.

Matthew's First Readers

Matthew does not describe its first readers. That was not necessary. They knew who they were and what they were up against. But scholars have learned how to use what Matthew says about Jesus, including what Jesus had said decades before,[1] to tell today's readers about the Gospel's first readers.

The intense efforts to do so, especially in recent decades, have produced an argument rather than a consensus. At issue is whether Matthew's first readers are to be seen as an embattled sect (or deviant group) *within* late first-century Judaism, or as an increasingly gentile church alienated from the Judaism in which it began.[2] This chapter assumes that the latter is the more likely. In any case, Matthew was not written to persuade synagogue Jews to become baptized disciples of Jesus.

Fortunately, there is wide agreement that Matthew was composed in about 95 CE. The implications of this date are more useful for understanding Matthew's first readers than knowing the anonymous Evangelist's address.[3]

The year 95 suggests the likelihood that some of the readers had been Christians for decades and perhaps had grown up hearing stories about Jesus and his teachings explained at home and in community worship. Exactly what they would have known can only be surmised since no one knows whether they had been using a copy of Mark, or of Q, or both (or neither). We may assume that what the readers found new was precisely Matthew's way of ordering and telling the Jesus stories and sayings, and its different wording of the already known. In any case, they would not have read this new account in order to acquire information about Jesus, so they could decide whether to become Christians; rather, they would have read Matthew to learn afresh what kind of Christian Jesus expects them to be.

In addition, those who first read Matthew in 95 CE did so 25 years after the Jewish war against Rome had decimated the church in Jerusalem and deprived the Jewish community of its central institution: the temple and its sacrifices offered by a hereditary priesthood. The Judaism that the readers saw was not the diverse religion of Jesus's day but a Judaism being redefined by a rabbinate appropriating the legacy of the prewar Pharisees and consolidating the community around the synagogue. Shortly before Matthew (in 85 CE) Gamaliel II apparently added to a synagogue prayer (the Eighteen Benedictions) a curse on "Nazarenes" and *Minim* (heretics), thereby making it impossible for them to remain bona fide members of the community. The curse's wording is not reported uniformly and its actual effectiveness unclear. What is clear are its targets: Jewish deviants, including Christian Jews, not all Christians. Like the synagogue, the church was asserting its distinct identity and defining its boundaries. Matthew's Jesus story is a significant part of this process.

Early Christian writings show that from the start, the figure of Jesus—his identity, his message, his meaning for life's ultimate questions—was central to the debates between synagogue and church. Inevitably, then, this loyalty to him affected what they said and sometimes wrote about him.

Given the situation of Matthew's first readers as well as the author's probable sources of information (see note 1), it is not surprising that Matthew is a complex narrative about a multifaceted, many-layered protagonist. Before examining its Christology, it is both prudent and rewarding to see how it is composed and to note how its Jesus is portrayed.

Matthew's Composition

A complex opening (1:1–4:16) and a compact conclusion (28:16–20) frame a running account whose turning point at 16:21 is reported simply, "from that time Jesus began to teach his disciples that he . . . must suffer . . . and be killed, and on the third day be raised." The narrative connects anecdotes that are sometimes stated in detail (e.g., 15:32–39), sometimes merely reported (as in 19:1–2). Rarely does the narrator explain how or why one incident led to the next. As a result,

Matthew's storyline consists of a series of scenes, linked by "and" or "then"—as do Mark's and Luke's.

What distinguishes Matthew's composition is the way it alternates between narrative and discourse. Five times the narrated action is arrested by Jesus's discourses, which assemble sayings derived largely from Q. Each discourse is outfitted with its own introduction and concluding comment, but none refers explicitly to another discourse or mentions what was reported in the narrative between them. Indeed, one could omit them without destroying the storyline; doing so would, however, drastically change both Matthew's image of Jesus and its Christology.

Each discourse is stitched into the narrative with a brief setting, noting Jesus's response (e.g., 4:23–5:2). A formulaic comment announces its completion (as in 7:28–29). Each discourse has its own theme: chapters 5–7 (the Sermon on the Mount) serve as Jesus's inaugural address, often announcing topics that will recur (e.g., 6:14–15 and 18:21–22). Chapter 10 instructs the disciples for their own mission and predicts what they will endure. Chapter 13 assembles parables to explain the various responses to Jesus's mission and message; chapter 18 gives guidance for the church's ethos, including disciplinary procedures. Chapters 24 and 25 (perhaps including chapter 23) concern the Great Judgment at the End. Though the discourses do not refer to each other, there is a logical thematic movement from one to the next. Especially noteworthy is the way each discourse's conclusion anticipates the theme that dominates the final discourse—the Last Judgment. That the five discourses are a deliberate counterpart to the Pentateuch (the five books of Moses) is not as obvious as is sometimes asserted.

Matthew's brief *conclusion* (28:16–20) implies the intended function of the Gospel. Here Jesus's unlimited authority,[4] presumably received from God at the resurrection, surpasses what the devil offered in the third temptation (4:8–9) and the authority Jesus had exercised in forgiving sins on earth (9:2–8); it also warrants the church's mission without relying on any of the Christological titles or images found in the rest of the Gospel. The name "Jesus" suffices (though some scholars unhesitatingly provide what is "missing"). The triadic baptismal formula in verse 19 is commonly regarded as that used in the author's church. Three observations must suffice.

Though Jesus had previously restricted his mission, and that of the disciples, to Israel's "lost sheep" (15:25) and had explicitly forbidden them to go to Samaritans and Gentiles (*ethnē*) as well (10:5–6), he now sends them to *all* the *ethnē* nations, "Gentiles" in the LXX). Israel is not mentioned (but is it included in "nations"?). Gentiles had appeared repeatedly in the narrative, beginning with the magi (2:1–2; 4:12–16; 8:5–13), and Jesus had foreseen the worldwide mission (24:14).

In chapter 10 the disciples' mission duplicates (and thus extends) that of Jesus: preach the Kingdom's imminence, heal the sick, raise the dead, cleanse lepers, and exorcise the demons. Now the task differs: "make disciples." (Apart from Acts 14:21, the verb *mathēteuein* occurs only here and 13:52; 27:57.) Their disciple-making has two aspects: baptism (marking entry into the church) and instruction. The surprising sequence is not accidental. Envisioned is not catechetical instruction leading to baptism, but *post*-baptismal; its content is not Christology and soteriology but the obligation to follow all that Jesus had enjoined or commanded—including the righteousness required at the Great Judgment. Given Matthew's emphasis on following Jesus, what is required should not be limited to what Jesus had said (grammatically) as imperatives. Rather, both Jesus's words and way alike are to be mandatory for the baptized disciple.

Jesus's promised presence until history's end recalls what the angel revealed in Joseph's dream: Mary's child would be called Emmanuel, meaning "God is with us" (1:23). Presumably the narrative will show how this was actualized in Jesus's mission. Similarly, what Jesus had promised in 18:20—that he would be present in even the smallest possible house church—is here extended to include the church dispersed in worldwide mission.[5] Jesus does not disclose *how* he will be present but suggests that he will be present where all that he had enjoined and exemplified is heeded. In short, he will be present where the Evangelist's narrative shapes church's life and work.

The *beginning* of the Matthean narrative (1:1–4:16) is quite different. Its horizon is not the future till the End but the past, stretching as far as Abraham, the "father" of Israel. One of its concerns is Jesus's significance grounded in his identity as both King David's son (descendant) *de jure* (by adoption) and God's Son *de facto* (by the virgin birth).

Matthew's prelude calls attention to "fulfillment" five times (1:22; 2:15, 17, 22; 4:12–14) by adding a formulaic expression to a report: "This happened to fulfill what was spoken by X, saying . . . " (The idea is expressed differently in 3:3.).[6] In 26:54–56 Jesus himself sees fulfillment of Scripture in his capture—the only time the claim is made to a disciple as well as to readers. Matthew does not explain or define "fulfillment" as a concept, for this was a common conviction of early Christians. Since the Greek *hina* can mean either purpose ("in order that") or result, in Matthew "fulfillment" probably announces that in the reported action the prophets' words, always true, became an actual event.

Logically, therefore, the act or event that fulfills is more significant (weightier) theologically than its verbalized counterpart in Scripture. In actualizing the previously spoken, Jesus's identity and activity confirmed the prophets' words without replacing or displacing them. (Not accidentally does the Christian Bible have two Testaments!) Jesus himself declares that he did not come to abolish Scripture but to fulfill it (5:17). In other words, because Scripture's words anticipate Jesus, he is its telos.

In addition to "fulfillment," Matthew's opening section contains other ways signaling what to look for in the narrative that follows. Fundamental is the angel's word in Joseph's first dream: Mary's son is to be named "Jesus, for he will save his people from their sins" (1:22),[7] not from the sins of others (i.e., the Romans). The identity of "his people" is not specified and should not be assumed; it will emerge as the account proceeds.

A significant clue to their identity appears in the baptizer's words about the Coming One as the thresher who, winnowing fork in hand, "will clear his threshing floor and gather his wheat into the granary, but the chaff he will burn" (3:12). In the imminent eschatological harvest, John's Jewish hearers cannot find security in their ethnic identity, for God can create Abraham's children from stones (3:9). In other words, saving "his people" will proceed by way of a sorting that distinguishes Jesus's community from everyone else.

Jesus himself asserted that he came to cause conflict and divide families (10:34–37) and distinguish his natural family from his true kin (12:48–50). He also contrasted the "infants" who received God's revelation and the "wise" who did not (11:6); the narrative contrasts the crowds' and the Pharisees's responses (9:33–38; 12:22–24; 15:29–31, etc.). However, after the narrative's hinge at 16:21, the Pharisees are regularly omitted from Jesus's true enemies, the priests (see 20:18; 26:3–5, 47, 59; 27:1,3,12; 28:12–15).

Thus, the tragic story of Herod's ordering the slaughter of Bethlehem's toddlers, coupled with its quotation of Jeremiah 31:15 (Rachel weeping over her dead children), serves as a dark cloud on the horizon, an ominous sign that the Jesus event will bring suffering to Israel.

As the patriarch Jacob's wife, Rachel is the "mother" of Israel. In Jeremiah, she weeps inconsolably over Israel's deportation to Babylon (31:15). Matthew, however, sees her lament as a foreshadow of the wretched situation after the disastrous war against Rome, viewed as God's punishment for the rejection of Jesus (see 21:33–46). Matthew does not, however, quote the very next verse (31:16) in which the Lord tells Rachel not to weep, for the exiles will return. What is unquoted should not be insinuated into Matthew's thought, for it is in Israel's negative response to Jesus that Jeremiah's words are "fulfilled." Various non-Christian Jewish texts also regarded the fall of Jerusalem as God's punishment for sin, though not the sin of refusing Jesus.[8]

Matthew's opening section also views the Jesus event through the lens of other biblical figures. Not only does Jesus remind the reader of Moses and Jeremiah, but John the Baptist too was prefigured—in Elijah (17:10–15).[9] Such "figural" reading of Scripture is alert to patterns in the biblical epic and sees in them marks of God's consistency and dependability, without thereby claiming that "history repeats itself."

The Jesus Portrayed

Matthew's Christology interprets the Jesus portrayed in the entire Gospel, in the narrative as a whole, not only in all its parts. This Christology's subject is not a "real Jesus" that historical critics construct "behind" the Gospel, though that Jesus too requires Christological analysis (as noted above).[10]

The more one reckons with the entire text (including what it does not say), the more complex and fascinating Matthew's picture of Jesus becomes. One finds both gaps in information and apparent duplications; logical inconsistencies—whether between teachings or between words and deeds—are allowed to stand without explanation or resolution. The Jesus who counsels loving enemies and prays for persecutors (5:44) is not said to do so himself (only in Luke does he pray for his crucifiers).

The tensions generated by the differences, divergences, or disparities in the portrayal of Jesus appear in three areas: the character of the man himself (including his self-awareness), his relation to his Jewish heritage, and the way he is related to his creation—the church.

Jesus and "His Church."[11] It is easier to say what the Evangelist did not understand by the word than to specify exactly what he had in mind when he had Jesus use it. In Matthew, it is neither Christ's "body," as it is for Paul (1 Corinthians 12:27), nor the "vine" and its branches, as in John 15:5, nor a "movement" determined to reform Judaism or change something in the world, as it is for some moderns today.

Rather, Matthew assumes that *ekklēsia* is the manifest consequence of what Jesus had done during his earthly mission, and still does, albeit in a different way. During that mission, he had said, "I will build my church," (16:18). The word is not used in the Great Commission (28:16–20), even though it sees baptism as marking entry into the church. In light of 16:18, the risen Christ's last word in Matthew implies that it is he, not the believers who actually "build" his *ekklēsia*. Accordingly, once Jesus's mission is underway, his followers are always part of the Jesus narrative.

Those Jesus called to "follow" do not merely accompany him; they are his "disciples," trainees in his way and thought. Though sometimes baffled by what they hear (19:25) and see (8:23–27), their experiences will often resemble his, for "a disciple is not above the teacher . . . it is enough for the disciple to be like the teacher" (18:24). In short, from this Evangelist's angle, separating "the church" from "the Jesus of history," as many critics have done, would distort the true picture because the real story of Jesus is the story of Jesus *and* the church.

Jesus's relation to his disciples, while never interrupted, is not idealized but portrayed realistically and is marked by Jesus's remarkable assurance as well as his devastating threats. A few quotations will show what is in view. In the chapter devoted to parables, Jesus assures the disciples that "the secrets [literally mysteries] of the kingdom of heaven" have been given to them but not to others. Indeed, "many prophets and righteous people longed to see what you see but did not see it, and hear what you hear but did not hear it" (13:11,17). Moreover, the disciples' privileged status is not only epistemological; it is also outfitted with saving power so effective that not even the gates of hades will be able to withstand it (16:18). Jesus views his followers as the earth's current salt and the world's light (5:13–15). He also promises that, at the Great Judgment "the righteous will shine like the sun in the kingdom of their Father" (13:43); that is, in effect he congratulates them as recipients of revelation, not as achievers of the rectitude required for admission to the kingdom. That verdict is reserved until the end, when, in the Son of Man's throne room, those who had cared for people deprived of food, clothing, health, and freedom will learn that they had been caring for Jesus himself (25:31–46).

Remarkable, therefore, is Jesus's warning: Though the disciples confess Jesus as Lord, exorcise demons, and do marvelous deeds in his name (as he asked them to do, 10:9), on judgment day he will repudiate them as evildoers (not mere slackers) whom he never knew in the first place, if they had not done the Father's will (7:21–23). Jesus does not explain why confessing him as Lord and doing good in his name do not qualify as doing what God wills. Instead, in the image of the two houses that concludes the Sermon on the Mount, he makes the peril vivid. Never does he promise mercy at the judgment.

Though Jesus is the Church's origin and *raison d'être*, it consists of flawed followers who are not excused from the judgment. At the end, the church will be as subject to winnowing as was Israel during Jesus's mission.

Jesus in "the house of Israel." Except for an unexplained foray to the Phoenician coast (15:20–28), the entire account of Jesus's mission takes place within "the house of Israel," among the Jewish people. His relation to his fellow Jews and to their shared religious heritage, however, deteriorates into mutual alienation and bitter hostility; the Jesus who foresaw his own death predicted Jerusalem's destruction as well.

His mission had an auspicious beginning in Galilee. He not only announced the message of the kingdom in "*their* synagogues," but also healed "every disease and sickness among the people." Consequently, "great crowds" followed him (4:23–25). Seeing them, he addressed his disciples with the Sermon on the Mount (5:1), thereby astonishing the crowds with his authority, unlike that of "*their* scribes" (7:28–29).

"*Their* scribes," like "*their* synagogues" (also 9:12; 10:17; 13:54), put distance between Jesus and his environment. In fact, the local synagogue was not his customary venue; it was elsewhere: the hills, the lake, a boat, and the streets and houses. Increasingly, synagogues are the place of confrontation and rejection even by his former neighbors whose unbelief shut down his healing activity (13:54–58). "*Their* synagogues" is where his disciples will be flogged (10:17). Nonetheless, Matthew's Jesus never faults the synagogue or the temple—the nation's sacred center—as such. His quarrel was not with these institutions but with the leaders and interpreters of the religious heritage who resist him and distort obedience to the Law.

The Evangelist tells the readers at the outset that Jesus's mission was light into darkness, not consummation of salvation history. In fact, it fulfilled Isaiah 9:2: "Light had dawned" for "the people who sat in darkness" (4:12–17). The placement of this claim implies that the stories that follow, whether of Jesus's conflicts with Pharisees or of his healings, make this light-into-darkness concrete as well as crucial for "the house of Israel."

Significant for Matthew's view of Jesus's relation to his fellow Jews is the treatment of Jesus and John the Baptist. Similarities are obvious: both operate within "the house of Israel," both fulfill words of Isaiah (3:3 and 12:15–21), and both call for repentance in response to the kingdom of heaven's imminence (3:2 and 4:17), and John, too, has disciples (11:2). Their similarities were even noted at the time: Some people, including Herod Antipas, regarded Jesus as another "John" (16:14; 14:2).

But their differences outweigh their similarities. Though Jesus's mission began when John's ended (4:12, 17), he is not portrayed as John's successor. Rather, John prepared the way for Jesus. Jesus himself saw him as the returned Elijah, expected to foreshadow his own role as the Son of Man (17:9–13). John and Jesus differed not only in apparel and diet (3:4) but also in style, substance, and significance. These differences, however, did not make one more acceptable than the other; rather, Israel refused both the ascetic baptizer and the hedonistic Nazarene (11:16–19). Further, though political rulers condemned both to death unjustly (14:3–12; 27:23–28), only Jesus's blood is said to effect forgiveness (26:28).[12]

Even though Jesus regarded John as the greatest man since Adam, "the least in the kingdom of heaven is greater" (11:11)—not because he is morally superior but because John marked the boundary between preparation and arrival—with Jesus's mission, the eschatology clock was beginning to strike high noon. Though both figures were the kingdom's heralds (3:2 and 4:17), only Jesus was also its harbinger, evidenced in his healings and exorcisms—none of which is reported of John, not said to be empowered by the Spirit as was Jesus.

In Matthew the cumulative differences between John and Jesus highlight and corroborate the view that Jesus is the event that climaxed God's dealings with Israel since Abraham (1:17). Together, the baptizer who does not heal and the healer who does not baptize summon the "house of Israel" to repentance, a decisive, definitive Godward turn— an invitation not to be spurned.

But spurned it was. Matthew's Jesus views his contemporaries as children who refuse to play funeral with John or wedding with himself (11:16–19). In return, Jesus never indulges the people's refusal by blaming extenuating circumstances nor does he accommodate a personal difficulty (see 18:21–22). He characterizes his contemporaries as an "evil and adulterous generation" (12:38–39, 43; 16:4), "faithless and perverse" (17:14–17), though "harassed and helpless, like sheep without a shepherd" (9:37). In 13:10–15 he explains why he speaks to them in parables: *They* have deliberately closed their eyes in order to avoid understanding and repenting. In fact, they "fulfilled" what Isaiah 6:9–10 foresaw:

> "*. . . they have shut their eyes;*
> *so that they might not look with their eyes,*
> *and listen with their ears,*
> *and understand with their heart and turn—*
> *and I would heal them.*"

Matthew, however, is not as harsh as Mark 4:11–12, where Jesus speaks in parables in order to produce this incomprehension!

But there is more. In Jerusalem, the tension between Jesus and his contemporaries escalates as he predicts the consequences of spurning his words and way (expressed already in Galilee, 8:11–12). The confrontation with the "chief priests and the scribes" that began on his first day in the city (21:1–17) grew only more bitter as he refused to explain his authorization, denounced them for not believing the baptizer, and used the parable of the wicked tenants to imply that God would replace them with more productive ones, as well suggest that God would also make him, the rejected stone, the keystone in a new structure (21:23–44). Only the crowds' view of Jesus "as a prophet" prevented the priests and Pharisees from promptly arresting him (21:45–46, alluding to verse 11).

The parable of the wedding banquet implies that God will destroy those who refused the invitation and burn their city (an allusion to what happened in 70 CE), as well as replace them with others, "both good and bad" (the imperfect church; see 13:47–50). Later, the crowds were persuaded to call for Barabbas's release and Jesus's crucifixion (27:15–23). Worse still, "the people as a whole" (NIV; "all the people,") took responsibility for it: "His blood be on us and on our children" (27:25). The latter phrase probably does not refer to all subsequent generations but to the one that would experience the disaster of 66–70 CE.

The clearer the entire storyline becomes, the greater the significance of what it does not contain: the silence about the political, national implications of Jesus as king (from birth!) and as Son of David by adoption (see above).

Both motifs appear in the story of Jesus's entering Jerusalem (21:1–1). As told, the event "fulfilled" the prophet's word (a combination of Isaiah 62:11 and Zecheriah 9:9): the king is coming to you, humble, and riding a donkey. The crowd acclaims the arrival of the Son of David, but then explains, "this is the prophet Jesus from Nazareth," not "this is the king of Israel."

Not only does the whole narrative lack marks of Jesus's royal status or its significance, but in the third temptation Jesus rejected kingly world power (4:8–11). The "triumphal" entry to Jerusalem is actually portrayed as a parody of a royal arrival. Nor do any of the frequent uses of Son of David imply or convey regal status; the title is regularly associated with healing, not kingship (9:27–30; 12:22–23; 15:22; 15:22; 20:29–31). In 22:41–45, Jesus himself questioned whether the Messiah is the Son of David, using Psalm 110:1: "The Lord said to my lord, 'Sit at my right hand.'"[13] Further, to Pilate's question "Are you the king of the Jews?" Jesus refuses a clear answer, and Matthew does not say that he was accused of this by the chief priests and elders. In this Gospel, Pilate did not have Jesus crucified as a subversive claimant to a throne but as an innocent victim of jealousy (27:11–14, 18). Implicitly, then, when the presumably gentile soldiers mocked Jesus with "Hail, King of the Jews," they mocked his opponents as well.

To sum up, Matthew's Jesus comes to "the house of Israel" as healer, provocative preacher of repentance, and as the Son of Man authorized to forgive sins on earth, not as a messianic Son of David or a king asserting his right to rule. Nor do his disciples plot or launch even a brief reach for political power; had they done so, they would have been arrested. Instead, Jesus compared his relation to his fellow Jews to a mother hen whose efforts to gather her chicks were rebuffed repeatedly; Jerusalem had a history of killing prophets (23:37–38).

But does not the fact that Jesus had *12* disciples (named in 10:2–4) symbolize the confederation of tribes that constituted Israel in biblical times? Yet nowhere does Matthew describe their roles as pillars of the church. Apart from their one-time Jesus-like mission (10:1), they have nothing special to do. And since we are not told that they traveled as a group, the symbolic significance of "12" was not part of Matthew's portrayal of their message. Nonetheless at the kingdom's arrival, when Jesus will be enthroned as Son of Man (not king), they will "sit on 12 thrones, judging the 12 tribes of Israel"—their reward for having left everything in order to follow Jesus (19:27–29). Whatever the Jesus of history may have had in mind, in Matthew this band of 12 is not seen as the administrative core of Jesus's theocratic earthly rule. "The 12" remains an unexplained given.

The Jesus portrayed *by* Matthew is *in* his environment but not really *of* it. He does not actually identify *with* the people or speak on their behalf; he has compassion *for* them, but he is sent *to* Israel's lost sheep. Inevitably, the more he articulates and embodies his grasp of the kingdom, the more he differs from what surrounds him; likewise, the nearer is the death destined for him, the more isolated he becomes— even from his disciples: one betrays, another denies, all "deserted him and fled" (26:56).

But what sort of person is it who dominates this narrative from beginning to end? The person portrayed is the subject of Matthew's Christology.

Jesus's Persona. Two features, together with traits already noted, mark this portrait: Jesus's use of supernatural power and his audacious teachings.

Though the author did not, like later patristic theologians, think in terms of Christ's two "natures," it would not distort Matthew's Christology to say that here Jesus's identity is both metaphysical and moral—that is, its supernatural character, asserted in the account of his origin and glimpsed in his miraculous deeds, implies a unique relation to nonphenomenal reality, and his passion for living rightly manifests his moral challenge to the human scene. Significantly, this duality in the portrait corresponds to Christology's two dimensions: the *theo*logical correlate and the anthropological/soteriological correlate, discussed in chapter 2.

That Jesus's *power* is supernatural is assumed throughout. It is implied in the disciples' question (after he had calmed a storm with a rebuke), "What kind of man is this?" (8:23–27); it is also acknowledged after he overcame gravity by walking on water and rescuing Peter from drowning, for the disciples worshipped him and confessed, "Truly, you are the Son of God" (14:25).

Commonly, his power is effective in his cures. His hand restores life to a dead girl, and merely touching his cloak evokes its healing capacity (9:20–25). Expelling a demon frees a mute's tongue (9:32–33). Yet his healing power can become ineffective in the absence of faith (13:58), and his foreknowledge of the future (apart from his death and resurrection) includes only its character, not its time (24:55). But he can also cause a fruitless fig tree to wither overnight (21:18–22).

The so-called "nature miracles on the lake" have overtones that symbolize Christ's presence and care for his church, especially in times of stress; the two stories of Jesus presiding over the feeding of two crowds suggest Christ's capacity to nourish his people. Even so, these stories are not treated like allegories, in which each item stands in for something else, as in the explanation of the parable of the soils (13:12–23).

For Jesus's persona, especially important is the way he used his power. That Jesus acts out of compassion is regularly implied and sometimes stated (14:14; 15:32). Never does he use this power for self-promotion, self-legitimization (12:38–39; 16:1–4), or self-protection.[14] Nor does Jesus's power need to be protected from contamination; being stronger than the demons and the maladies to be healed, he can touch the lepers and command the demonic to leave (8:2–3; 9:20–25; 28–30; 14:35–36; 20:34). In short, Matthew portrays Jesus as harsh toward those who refuse him (e.g., 11:20–24), but consistently compassionate toward those who need him—unlike the baptizer who is never said to have compassion.

The audacity of the *teaching* Jesus, Matthew points out, did not go unnoticed at the time. After the Sermon on the Mount concluded, "the crowds were astounded at his teaching, for he taught them as one having authority, and not as their scribes" (7:28–29). In the Gospel, the difference appears in what he says and how he says it. He cites neither precedent nor eminent teachers, as scribes did (and scholars still do) to support his pronouncements. For instance, without hesitation, he rejects defilement (religious impurity) as contamination and redefines it in moral terms: "evil intentions, murder, adultery, fornication, theft, false witness, slander" (many of these he had already redefined in 5:21–48). These acts defile the *person* because they come from the heart, the self's animating moral center. Food, on the other hand, enters only the stomach and then "goes out into the sewer." So what really defiles is what comes *out* of the mouth (15:1–20; Matthew omits Mark 7:9: "thus he declared all foods clean").

Jesus's astounding self-confidence is a symptom of his sense of authorization, evident from the first Beatitude, in which he knows to whom God's kingdom belongs (5:3), to his final word, in which he asserts his impending rule as the Son of Man at God's right hand (26:63). In addition, by including the so-called "antitheses" in the Sermon on the Mount (5:21–48), the Evangelist astutely made their sixfold "you have heard . . . but I say" the rubric over Jesus's teaching in the rest of the Gospel as well.

The character of the Sermon on the Mount is also a factor in prompting the comment about the crowds' astonishment, though the Gospel writer does not point it out. To begin with, as an aggregate of sayings formed into an uninterrupted torrent of remarkable assertions, the Sermon makes a more powerful impact on the listening crowd (and reader) than its teachings would make individually. The impact of the whole is cumulative, and its intensity accelerates as the Sermon moves relentlessly toward its final warning. Moreover, in being assembled into the Sermon, every teaching has been shorn of its local setting or triggering circumstances (as retained in 15:1–20). As a result, the Sermon, by making no allowance for extenuating situations in the hearer's life, has an absolutist tone, like apodictic law, which simply declares what is required and prohibited, full stop. In this Sermon, Jesus does not encourage his audiences with "do the best you can," but confronts them with "be perfect as your heavenly Father is perfect" (5:48).

Also, in creating the Sermon, the Evangelist provided the whole with a specific setting: the message and mission of Jesus as summarized in 4:23–25. The meaning of the Sermon's content is now tied to and contingent on him. Its validity is anchored in his identity; it gives him the right to assert "You have heard . . . but I say to you." In short, the Sermon is more than a moral manifesto; it is also a Christological statement. Matthew's Jesus knows who he is and what he must do. On more than one occasion he did not hesitate to say so.

In a passage discussed below, Jesus thanks God for hiding "these things" from "the wise" and revealing them to "infants" instead (11:25–26). Indeed, this two-sided result was God's "gracious will." In this remarkable passage, Jesus also declares himself to be the sole person qualified to reveal God and the only one whose mode of being ("yoke") can relieve the wearied of burdensome existence.[15] Again and again, in one setting after another and expressed in one idiom or other, the Matthean Jesus implies, asserts, or insists that he alone is, and must be, central. This persona is free of hesitation and doubt, self-doubt included. Likewise, his speech lacks caution, nor does he protect it by adding qualifiers to it, such as *probably, perhaps, usually, on the whole,* or *it seems likely.* They would have compromised his bold authority and modified his significance, which surpasses that of King Solomon or the temple (12:42). So, too, Jesus's confidence is not said or shown to have developed. This trait of this particular persona is simply there, a "given" that is as unavoidable as it is unmistakable.

Seen as a whole, Matthew—despite its various promises and assurances—is a joyless narrative about a joyless Jesus who urges his persecuted followers to rejoice (5:11–12) but is never said to have done so himself. This is an utterly serious Jesus who expects to be taken seriously. This Jesus is visualizable as the Christ of many mosaics in Byzantine church—a stern persona who is to be obeyed.

The Anthropological/Soteriological Correlate

The Human Condition Addressed

That Matthew does not summarize its view of the human condition should not surprise us; after all, its Jesus was not a systematic thinker given to explaining concepts. This healer/teacher/preacher addressed certain aspects of the human plight with his amazing deeds as well as bold assertions and admonitions, vivid parables, and predictions. By instantiating his general call to repentance with specific requirements, moreover, he identified essential features of the human condition and also made repentance its urgent remedy.[16]

Understanding this anthropology of repentance requires attending to the logic of the concept itself, to the nature of self, and to the power of hypocrisy to corrupt even the good actually done.

The essence of repentance (*metanoia*) is neither remorse for wrongs done or good not done, nor penance—punishment, prescribed or self-inflicted for acknowledged guilt. Etymologically, *metanoia* means "mind change," but its more biblical meaning accents moral change.[17] This meaning reflects the Hebrew *teshubah* ("turning") retained in the English "conversion" and "convert" and the German *Bekehrung* (from *kehr*, "to turn"). Repentance implies change. Jesus's call to repent is his response to the nearness of God's reign, to the kind of reality created when God's will is done on earth as it is in heaven. In other words, what Jesus calls for is turning life resolutely *toward* God's character, fully actualized and *away from* whatever must be abandoned if that reign is to be complete, unchallenged, and transformative.

The fact that repentance is the central theme of Jesus's entire message and mission implies that for him life is otherwise awry, distorted, or thwarted because it does not correspond to God's will and way; moreover, it will stay that way until it is turned Godward, aligned rightly, and held that way. The Matthean Jesus does not *teach* a doctrine of "original sin" or insist on the ubiquity of sin. He simply assumes that everyone he encounters needs to repent and that the hearer can do so. No one responds to Jesus by saying what Paul confesses, "I can will what is right, but I cannot do it," or its equivalent opposite, "I do not do the good I want, but the evil I do not want" (Romans 7:18–19). What we hear Paul say, however, we see happen in Matthew 19:16–22. Here a wealthy youth, lifelong Torah observant, cannot become a disciple because he is unwilling to exchange his possessions on earth for treasures in heaven by selling them and giving the proceeds to the poor.

Characteristically, the Matthean Jesus holds the individual accountable for the character and direction of one's life. In doing so, he implicitly regards the brutal social and economic realities of his environment as symptoms of the human condition, not its causes. Though his imagery mentions torture for defaulting repayment of a loan (18:39), debtor's imprisonment (5:25–26), compulsory service and begging (5:41–42), unemployed day laborers (20:1–16), wealthy absentee landlords and their tenants (21:33–34), he nowhere blames "the system" or Rome for maintaining it. Nor are such harsh realities seen as extenuating circumstances that excuse the self's refusal to repent. Rather, he accosts the self *in* such circumstances, not the circumstances themselves. The self can repent despite its circumstances. They do, however, often make the Godward turn costly.

The devil's role in the human condition is ambiguous in Matthew. On the one hand, the interpretation of the parable of the weeds in the wheat field, found only in Matthew 13:24–30, 36–43, makes the devil responsible for the existence of evildoers in the church. On the other hand, in the parable of the soils (13:1–23) the seed that fell on the path is eaten by birds—that is, "the evil one comes to take it away." He is not blamed, however, when the sprouted seed withers in the hot sun (persecution) or when a patch of thorns (wealth) chokes the Word. Nor is the devil the instigator of the persecutions foreseen in chapter 10 and in 24:9–13, or of false prophets and false messiahs in 24:11, 24, or of the "increase of wickedness" that will cause most people's love to "grow cold" (24:12). Matthew 26:17 does not, like Luke 22:3, blame Satan for Judas's betrayal of Jesus. Nor does Matthew anywhere suggest that Jesus's exorcisms imply that the human condition as a whole is demon driven. Matthew's dualism is not Manichean.

Holding the individual accountable implies that if one's life is to be lived Godward, true repentance must begin in the heart. It is here, at the self's inner invisible center, that one's antagonisms and allegiances, denials and dispositions, anxieties and aspirations contend and thereby determine one's identity and generate the acts of the external, visible self. In emphasizing the nonapparent inner self Jesus does not let piety eclipse moral action; that he rather facilitates it is clear in his unusual command, "first cleanse the inside of the cup so that the outside also may become clean" (23:26). So, too, good fruit attests the health of the tree that produces it (7:17–18).

Likewise, "it is not what goes into the mouth that defiles a person, but . . . what comes out" (15:11). So, too, adultery occurs first in the heart (5:28). Evil people cannot speak good things because the mouth speaks what is in the heart (12:34). Not surprisingly the first commandment calls for loving God with one's entire inner self ("with all your heart . . . soul . . . self," 22:37–39). Where such uncompromised, unambivalent love for God exists, the self is truly turned Godward, and the cup's exterior manifests its inner cleanness.

What provokes Jesus's harshest criticism is hypocrisy: the contradiction between the self's actual state and the person's deliberately projected image. Neither Jesus nor the Evangelist defines the word or describes its corrosive effects on the self's integrity. Nor need we surmise what motivated Jesus to emphasize hypocrisy so strongly and in so many ways. What matters is grasping the significance of hypocrisy for the human condition.

Though Jesus uses the word *hypokrisis* only once (23:27–28), he exposes the phenomenon repeatedly and variously, most often by denouncing the scribes and Pharisees as *hypokritai*. Two passages show what hypocrisy entails. In 15:3–9 Jesus applied to his critics what Isaiah had said long before about the nation: "this people honor me with their lips, but their hearts are far from me" (Isaiah 29:13).[18] Matthew's Jesus never accuses the people as a whole of hypocrisy, nor does he view the Pharisees as representing the Jewish religion; in his eyes, they misrepresent it.

In the second passage (23:3) Jesus tells his disciples to follow the Pharisees' teaching but not their deeds. It is not the ordinary difference between good intent and flawed result, between avowed ideal and imperfect attainment that Jesus exposes, but the actual contradiction between word and deed that one conceals from others. Hypocrites are whitewashed tombs, made externally beautiful but internally full of death and filth (23:27–29). Indeed, by quoting Isaiah, Jesus implies that hypocrisy corrodes and annuls one's worship of God as well.

For Jesus, hypocrisy is not a specific act, a transgression. Rather, it names a malign state of affairs that exists when what is true of the self's core, the state of the heart, contradicts the image being projected by apparently righteous behavior. This contradiction, moreover, deludes both the self and the observer; both take the image for reality. So serious is hypocrisy that the convert to Pharisaism is twice as deluded as the Pharisee (23:15). The hypocrite is a blind guide (23:6) and falls into the same pit as the one guided (15:15). Self-delusion can take many forms, as when one volunteers to remove the speck in another's eye while ignoring the vision-impairing mass in one's own (7:3–5). It is manifest in those who devoutly decorate martyrs' tombs while saying proudly, "Had *we* lived then, we would not have shed their blood" (23:29–30). Jesus also detects hypocrisy when religious practices, valid in themselves, are skewed morally because matters like justice (*krisin*, judgment), mercy, and faith are neglected and minutiae are emphasized instead; where that occurs, the gnat is strained out, but the camel is swallowed (23:23–24).

Hypocrisy, not being generated by a religion's finitude or flaws but by an unexplained propensity of the heart, distorts one's relation to God. It cannot, therefore, be eradicated by adopting certain religious practices, whether more relaxed or more rigorous. Overcoming hypocrisy entails doing what Jesus's message calls for: turning the self-aggrandizing heart to look Godward for direction and vindication. Jesus implies this antidote in the sayings that frame the Lord's prayer: for hypocrites who want their righteous deeds (NRSV: piety) to be seen and approved, current public approbation *is* their validation. But the Godward self that acts secretly counts on God for validation in the future (6:1–6, 16–18). Implicitly, then, it is the hypocrisy-free righteousness of the Godward self that "exceeds" the righteousness of the scribes and Pharisees that Jesus mandates (5:20). In short, righteousness is the exact opposite of hypocrisy. Examining the Godward-turned life as the soteriological antidote to the human condition is therefore the next step.

The Righteous Life Designed

Matthew's view of the Godward life, like its understanding of the human condition, must be constructed by probing what the Matthean Jesus assumes, asserts, and requires, as well as what he does not say. The sharpest—and most challenging—profile of the Godward life appears in the Sermon on the Mount. Three aspects of the envisioned life will be noted: the redefined righteousness, the ethos of forgiveness, and the role of the righteous Jesus.

The core meaning of the word *righteousness* is rightness, rectitude. Rightness always implies a norm, a standard, an accepted criterion by which a thing, an act, a state of affairs, or a person is judged to be what it ought to be in that specific context.

The noun "righteousness" renders *dikaiosynē*; the adjective "righteous" translates *dikaios*; the verb *dikaioun* is rare in Matthew but fundamental in Paul's Romans. *Dikaiosynē* can also be translated "justice," but Bible translations usually prefer the Germanic "righteousness" (see *Gerechtigkeit*, the quality of being right), not the more juridical Latinate "justice" (see *justitia*).

The core meaning accounts for some unexpected usages. Thus Deuteronomy 25:15 says weights and measures are "righteous" because they are correct. Deeds are "righteous" when they accord with the appropriate norm in a given context. In the Old Testament, the prevailing context is the covenant—a compact unilaterally initiated by God that has bilateral obligations between God and Israel. So Judges 5:11 can call Israel's military victories God's "righteousnesses" because in them God did what was right for the covenant partner. Similarly, in Isaiah 51:5 "my righteousness" refers to God's act of returning Israelite exiles from Babylon. In juridical contexts, actual or figural "righteous" takes on a forensic meaning: the accused is declared "righteous" (i.e., acquitted) because he is in the right, not because he is good. In early

Judaism, rabbis used the plural *tsidqoth* to speak of deeds of charity, the right thing to do. At Qumran, the founder of the community was called the Teacher of Righteousness, because he either taught it or was a person with rectitude, or both.

The word *dikaiosyē* appears seven times (3:15, 5:6, 10, 20; 6:1, 33; 21:32), always in a passage peculiar to Matthew. As the first thing the Matthean Jesus says, it asserts that John's baptizing Jesus is the proper way for both "to fulfill all righteousness" (3:15); it accords completely with God's will by completing John's preparatory role and by pointing to what the Jesus event will be about. As the narrative nears its climax, (only) Matthew reports that during Jesus's civil trial Pilate received a message from his distraught wife, urging him to have nothing to do with "that righteous man" (27:19).[19] What 3:15 anticipates, 27:19 affirms—the narrative in between is an account of the righteous Jesus.

Matthew is not an account of how Jesus became a righteous person; it is not a *Bildungsroman*. The subject matter of Jesus's teaching is not his own character development, or source of his own righteousness; it is rather the righteousness of others, and what perverts or prevents it. It is precisely this other-oriented trait that makes the Matthean Jesus's view of rightness soteriologically significant. In accordance with the framework of the Lord's Prayer, Jesus manifests his righteousness partly by not claiming to be righteous.

Just as Matthew's Jesus can instantiate repentance and expose hypocrisy without mentioning the words themselves, so he can make his understanding of righteousness clear with other language. However, it is precisely the formal definition of righteousness—the right alignment with the proper norm—that allows one to see the same subject matter expressed in various ways, and thereby to think theologically.

According to the fourth Beatitude (5:6) righteousness is not a presently enjoyed state; it is rather a good whose painful dearth is imaged as yearning for life's necessities—food and drink. Yet it is precisely these deprived who are "blessed" because their famished, empty, selves will be amply filled, or sated. In this Beatitude (as in the second and seventh) the future passive form of the verbs implies that God is the doer, the one who will provide righteousness prodigiously, who will give mercy to the currently merciful, and who will regard peacemakers as children of God. At the present, however, the Godward are being persecuted "for righteousness sake" (5:10)—that is, because their form of rectitude provokes opposition. Even so, God's kingdom "belongs" to them (presumably because they have responded to its character by turning Godward), as it does to those whose "spirit" is impoverished (depressed; 5:3). In other words, according to the plot, scripted by God, salvation is experienced now as God's anticipated, dependable, nevertheless. Those turned Godward can count on it. Indeed, this steady Godward turning and counting on God amount to the same thing as 6:1–18 makes clear. Yearning passionately for rightness is not in vain. The righteousness that evokes persecution now is vindicated at the End.

The righteousness that "exceeds" that of the scribes and Pharisees (5:20) is not defined, but in 5:44–47 its differentiating character is shown by examples and its import is summarized in verse 48: "Be perfect . . . as your heavenly Father is perfect." Formally, this mandated *imago dei* resembles the demand that Israel be holy because God is holy (Leviticus 19:2), but materially it differs subtly: law-normed scribal rectitude is surpassed by a rectitude that mirrors the Father's character directly—that is, without being refracted through exegesis of a text. The difference between these two modes of righteousness is signaled six times by a formulaic rubric set over diverse sayings: "you have heard that it was said [in Scripture, or was thought to be said, verse 43] . . . but I say to you."

Seeing the Christological significance of 5:17–48 as a whole requires more than understanding what Jesus is saying in each of its parts; also required is comprehending what he is doing by saying all of these things together. Jesus is defining the righteousness required for admission to the kingdom of heaven (5:20) by redefining obedience to what Scripture says. He was also showing himself as Scripture's definitive interpreter. When he cites Scriptures and then adds, "but I say to you," Jesus is neither displacing nor replacing Scripture, nor is he contradicting his own insistence that he came to "fulfill" it (5:17). Rather, he is stating concretely what he came to do. As a result, in the six instantiations of the redefined rectitude, the morally right thing to do always "exceeds" compliance (the legally right thing to do), for it accords with the heart of the self turned Godward in response to the character of God's kingly reign.

Further, because the Jesus rectitude is the passport to the kingdom of heaven, it also indicates the kind of impact the righteous Jesus has on those who heed his words and follow his way. The commands that follow each "but I say" were probably selected to exemplify the behavior that results from a change in the heart. The Sermon's view of the disciple's life discloses, therefore, formative features of Jesus's religious significance according to Matthew. Put simply, in saving "his people from their sins" (1:21), Jesus saves individuals from their transgressions without changing the ontic structure of existence itself. Disciples are still mortal. Nor does he save them by creating a conventicle of the righteous (as attempted at Qumran and numberless places since). He saves them in the human condition by breaking its power in the heart.

The Godward life, as portrayed in these striking concretions, is not particularly "religious": Jesus does not baptize or emphasize the sacred sacrifices in the temple. Nonetheless, because the Godward life takes its shape and derives its power from the character of God's reign, Jesus's commands are absolute, not circumstantial. The rectitude that accords with God's reign is neither prudential (it evokes persecution, not approbation), nor is it transactional (calculating cost/benefits). These commands are not ideals that would improve the world if only more people followed them (true as that may be). All such considerations are foreign to the Sermon. It does not promise that loving will turn the enemy into a friend. The "benefit" of obeying Jesus accrues to the doer, not to the recipient of the good deed. These things ought to be done because responding rightly to the reality of God's reign calls for such action. Full stop.

In addition to redefining rightness as unalloyed, unhypocritical rectitude flowing from the heart turned Godward, the Matthean Jesus also enjoins an ethos of *forgiveness*, beginning with the Sermon on the Mount.[20]

By including forgiveness in the Lord's Prayer (6:9), the Matthean Jesus implies that asking for (and receiving) God's forgiveness, together with forgiving others, is a fundamental feature of the Godward life, not an occasional experience. The link between being forgiven and forgiving is decisive. Later, in the discourse concerned with inner-church affairs, Jesus doubles down on the same point: He tells Peter that there is no limit to the number of times he must forgive the same fellow Christian (18:21–22). There follows the parable of the slave who is forgiven an enormous debt but then refuses to forgive a paltry one, and so forfeits his own forgiveness and is punished mercilessly as well.

One looks in vain for Matthew's definition of forgiveness, but its logic can illumine the subject. To begin with, forgiveness is a way of correcting a soured, distorted, abused, or violated relationship between persons who normally know one another. Forgiveness assumes that someone has done (or neglected to do) something that offends the other party, whether a social equal ("brother" in 18:25, fellow slave in 18:28) or unequal (a king and his slave in 18:24).

Further, forgiveness does not change what happened or excuse it; it changes the *impact* of the offender's actions (or inaction). In forgiveness, the negative impact no longer controls the future of both the offender and the offended: the former ceases to be treated as a culprit; the latter is no longer controlled by resentment and retaliation. This liberation does not trivialize the wrong deed or explain it as ignorance or moral inability, nor does it exonerate the offender by emphasizing extenuating circumstances. To the contrary, forgiveness takes one's deeds and their consequences for the other with genuine seriousness.

Also, forgiveness is a generous act of the offended toward the offender. In forgiving, the aggrieved person forgoes the right to "get even," to retaliate, to compel legitimate compliance with what is proper. In forgiving, the offended does the unwarranted. Forgiveness, then, is neither transactional (a cost–benefit calculation) nor a reward (for the offender's deepest regret or subsequent good behavior). Forgiveness is a gift, an act of grace; it cannot be earned. It can, however, be forfeited by taking it for granted.

These observations suggest that forgiveness was more characteristic of Jesus's whole mission than the unique story in 9:2–8 implies— *if* one recognizes the traits of forgiveness in his actions. Thus, he embodies forgiveness when he "called" a usually despised tax collector (Matthew) and then dined with his peers and other "sinners" (9:9–10). So, too, he actualized forgiveness in not treating his disciples as they had treated him on Good Friday. Some of his requirements also entail forgiveness—for example, turning the other cheek toward the aggressor (5:38–39) and praying for the persecutor's well-being (5:43–44).

The third element in the design of the righteous life is *the impact of the righteous Jesus* on the life of his forgiven followers. This, it turns out, is the way Jesus, the embodiment and exemplar of true righteousness, becomes the enabler of righteousness in others.[21]

The word "disciple" (*mathētēs*) distinguishes one kind of learner from other kinds (e.g., the student, the researcher, the expert, the experimenter) by emphasizing a particular *mode* of learning: Instead of memorizing, investigating, or assimilating new data, the disciple learns by deliberate attachment to a specific teacher—for example, an aspiring singer goes to an eminent voice teacher. "Disciple learning" occurs by the intentional bond created between the teacher and the learner. The disciple learns by attending to the teacher's thoughts, ways, skills, habits, and attitudes in order to make the master's wisdom one's own. In Matthew, it is the risen Jesus's command, "make disciples" (28:19) that endows his original followers' own relation to him with special significance for later generations.

The "call" stories do more than explain how Jesus acquired disciples. In none of the terse reports (4:12–22; 9:9) do the men find their teacher; rather, he finds them, interrupts their work, and summons them to "follow." They obey promptly (as Peter later reminds Jesus, "Look, we have left everything and followed you" [19:27]). This response is paradigmatic.

The band of disciples, however, forms a "fictive family" (12.48–50) that is to be nonhierarchical: none of them is to be "above" the others; they are all learners of the one teacher (23:8–10). Nor should they expect to become teachers with their own disciples. The goal is not to become independent of the teacher but to be like him (10:24–25). Indeed, "whoever wishes to be great among you must be your servant . . . just as the Son of Man came not to be served but to serve, and to give his life a ransom for many" (20:26–28). Indeed, the disciples must "deny themselves and take up *their* cross and follow me" (16:24), not Jesus's cross. His cross needs neither completion nor duplication; it needs appropriation as the empowering image of a way of life shaped intentionally and persistently by allegiance to Jesus.

At the same time Matthew eschews describing the details of Jesus's private life that might tempt a devotee to duplicate the master literally. Compared to what 3:4 says about the baptizer, nothing is reported about Jesus's diet and dress; we learn nothing of his idiosyncrasies or sexuality. Absent also is any interest in pilgrimages to places where Jesus had done amazing things. Being a disciple calls rather for an energizing, risky, and often costly struggle of the self with the self.

In declaring, "It is enough for the disciple to be like the teacher, and the slave like the master" (10:25), Jesus identifies discipleship as the means by which the righteous Jesus effects righteousness in others—without, however, explaining exactly how this happens. Matthew neither says nor shows how the Twelve gradually become more righteous by walking, sailing, eating, and talking daily with Jesus. Nor does the Gospel romanticize their time with him as idealized individual disciples (as the Fourth Gospel does with its "beloved disciple").

The Twelve are not portrayed as models to follow, for they often seem to stumble behind Jesus.

In 13:51 the disciples claim they understand Jesus's parabolic language, but in 16:5–12 he chides them for not understanding it. Soon after, their spokesman is commended for making the right Christological confession but then is repudiated for misunderstanding it (16:13–23). Jesus is disappointed by their "little faith" (14:11; 12:19–20) and dismayed by their sleeping in Gethsemane, while he prays his heart out (26:40–46). Having claimed to understand what they heard, they misunderstand the transfiguration that they see (17:1–8). In Jerusalem, these Galileans point out the sights to Jesus who foresees only their destruction (26:31–35).

The Theological Correlate

Historian Robert Wilken was on target when he observed that by inviting people to become his disciples, Jesus "made himself part of his message."[22] In 11:28–30 Jesus put it this way: "Come to me all you that are weary . . . and I will give you rest. Take my yoke . . . and learn from me, for I am gentle and . . . my yoke is easy." But what, in Matthew, warrants this audacious fusion of man and message? According to 13:54–57, Jesus's erstwhile neighbors, who knew his whole family, asked the same question: "Where did this man get all this?" The answer: Jesus's relation to God, the content of Christology's theological correlate.

The Son and His Father
While some aspect of Jesus's relation to God is implicit throughout Matthew's entire narrative, some passages are explicitly theological: they state Jesus's theological identity or his religious significance. Surprisingly, even such passages leave much unsaid and do not refer to each other.

In 20:28, Jesus's death is a "ransom for many," and in 26:28 it secured "the forgiveness of sins" for many; neither assertion explains or links these passages or makes Jesus's relation to God explicit. Likewise, Jesus's three "passion predictions" mention neither the salvific purpose of his death nor God's role in it. The second and third (17:22–23; 20:17–19) simply foresee what will happen to him; the first (16:21) asserts only that he "must" go to Jerusalem to be killed. This "must" is not a historical inevitability, set in motion by the plotting against him; (12:14), it is an unexplained theological necessity.

In Matthew, neither the king's court nor the priest's altar provides the vocabulary and imagery for expressing Jesus's relation to God, but the language of the family: father and son. Such language is appropriate for the subject because each term implies the other, even when only one of them is used. Consequently, this Christology's theological correlate is formulated aptly and concisely by the phrase "Son of God." Looking briefly at *how "Son of God" is used* can focus this discussion.

To begin with, of the many "titles" applied to Jesus in Matthew, only "Son of God" overarches and frames the whole narrative, from the virgin birth to the death on the cross. (The virgin birth implies that Jesus did not "become" God's son but was so from the beginning of his earthly existence.) At the end, the Roman soldiers declare, "Truly this man was God's Son!" (27:54). As the comprehensive category, "Son of God" modifies and interprets Matthew's other ways of saying who Jesus was and why he matters. Nonetheless, the narrator himself never uses the title in his own comments, though it is pivotal in many of his stories. The subject of his verbs is never "The Son of God" but simply "Jesus." The title—used in confession, taunt, accusation, or amazement—appears in the mouth of the devil and demons (4:3, 6; 8:29, respectively), as well as on the lips of humans: disciples (14:33; 16:16), the high priest (26:63), and mockers at the crucifixion (27:40).

That "Son of God" refers primarily to the Jesus–God relation rather than to Jesus's "divinity" as such is shown by the fact that both Jesus and God refer to each other in the same familial language. On the one hand, twice God's voice explicitly calls Jesus "my Son" (at the baptism and at the transfiguration, 3:17 and 17:5).

On the other hand, Jesus consistently and characteristically speaks of God as "my (or "my heavenly") Father." However, when speaking of the disciples' relation to God, he always uses "your Father," thereby tacitly distinguishing his own relation to God from theirs. Accordingly, only in the Lord's Prayer (used by the community) does he use "our Father," thereby implying that his God relationship could be shared because he is "*The* Son" (11:27; also 24:36), not as one of the brothers who have the same parent.[23]

Matthew implies that Jesus knew his relation to God was unique since he *heard* the voice and "*saw* the Spirit of God descending . . . and alighting on him" (3:16). Moreover, given the Spirit's role also in his conception, the whole Jesus-event, man and mission alike, is tacitly shown to be affected and energized by God's power or Spirit.

In Matthew's account, two witnesses attest the role of the Spirit in Jesus's mission: the narrator and Jesus himself. In 12:15–21, it is the narrator who points out that Jesus's multiple cures fulfill God's promise to give his Spirit to his servant, stated in Isa 42:1–4, the longest biblical quotation in this Gospel.[24] In 12:28 Jesus asserts that expelling demons by God's Spirit brings God's kingdom to those freed. Here Jesus also declares that every sin and blasphemy is forgivable (by God) except blasphemy against the Spirit (his God-given link to God).

But the Spirit-endowed Jesus did not undertake his lifework immediately. He first had to discern what being God's "Son" precluded and required. So Jesus, led by the Spirit that empowered him and hungering after a 40-day fast that weakened him, learned what "Son of God" really means through a three-dimensional encounter with the devil himself (4:1–11). Though Matthew's Jesus never mentions this experience, for Matthew (and therefore its readers as well) its contours presaged and determined the character of the rest of the Jesus event.

The three scenes reported in 4:1–11 do not depict the temptation experiences themselves; they show the issues and Jesus's reliance on texts in Deuteronomy to thwart the devil's lures. In quoting what God says in Scripture, Jesus shows himself to be the obedient Son.

Increasingly, each scene lures Jesus to see opportunities in his status as God's Spirit-empowered Son.

The famished Jesus is first tempted to preserve himself by turning stones into bread. But according to Deuteronomy 8:3, what really sustains life is God's word. But God's word also prompts the next temptation: since Psalm 91:11–12 (quoted by the devil!) promises God's protection, why not leap from the temple to show everyone that God is trustworthy? Deuteronomy 6:16, however, forbids testing God's reliability. Finally, Jesus is offered a specious bargain: He can exercise full political power and enjoy its splendor—his due as God's Son—by granting that on earth the devil has the last word. Deuteronomy 6:13, however, forbids compromising the worship of God alone.

In various ways, Matthew's subsequent narrative confirms Jesus's successful encounter with the devil. For instance, having refused to use his power to feed himself, he fed multitudes twice. Having refused to demonstrate God's protection, at his arrest he asked, "Do you think I cannot appeal to my Father, and he will send me more than twelve legions of angels (to rescue me)?" In Peter's objection to the necessity of death Jesus heard the voice of Satan again. In short, in rebuffing the devil Jesus established his freedom from the hypocrisy inherent in each temptation, as well as his determination to be the Father's obedient Son. The baptism and temptation stories tell us what happened at the outset; they also point us to what we should look for in the narrative to follow.

Had the Evangelist, like the author of Mark, simply reported *that* Jesus was tempted by the devil, the Matthean Jesus would have projected a different image. He would have been a Spirit-begotten, Spirit-empowered figure who is spared the struggle to understand what his unique identity did and did not call for. Further, Jesus's relation to God would then have been determined solely by the uniqueness of his nature instead of by the determination of his will as well. Above all, such a Jesus would have lacked the moral authority that was gained by his deliberate obedience to God's will in Scripture. But it was the power of his own obedience that gave him the moral right—as distinct from the ontological right—to summon his first disciples to abandon work and family in order to follow him unreservedly, and to redefine righteousness by stating God's character afresh.

So, then, the title "Son of God" itself does not really say who Jesus is; it is rather Jesus's obedience—its shape and cost—that actually discloses the meaning of the title. Apart from the meaning he gives it, it remains ambiguous in the history of religion and often misleading in the thought of devoted followers—as Peter found out when Jesus rebuked him.

As the obedient Son, Jesus acts as *God's emissary*, expressed in Jesus's talk of being "sent" as well as having "come."

In 10:40 he tells the disciples, "Whoever welcomes you welcomes me, and whoever welcomes me welcomes the one who sent me." In 15:24 he says he was sent only to Israel's lost sheep. In the allegorical Christology parable (21:33–45) the tenants kill the sent son. Jesus also speaks of himself as having "come" (i.e., arrived on the scene) in 5:17; 9:13; 10:34–35, each time correcting a wrong view of his mission

That Jesus was sent by God seems self-evident in Matthew; that he did not "come" from Nazareth is obvious as well; that the Evangelist was reluctant to say explicitly that Jesus was sent by God or came from heaven is unlikely. That those verbs imply the preexistence of the sent/arrived Son is perhaps possible.[25] Be that as it may, Jesus's claim to be "sent" implies that he does not see himself as a volunteer in God's service, but as an agent tasked and empowered to do the sender's will. That God's emissary will act like God is signaled in 1:28 when the angel tells Joseph that Mary's child will be "Emmanuel," in Hebrew: "God is with us."

Jesus is shown exercising power over nature. In calming a storm, he does what God does: "you rule the raging of the sea, when its waves rise, you still them" (Psalm 89:9). Jesus himself uses the language of Isa 35:5–6, celebrating *God's* coming to save, to interpret his own cures and exorcisms. Further, as the Son of Man on earth, Jesus forgives sins (9:6) and calls "sinners"—actions in accord with God's desire for mercy among humans (9:13). Jesus's indiscriminate eating also with tax collectors and sinners echoes God's sending sun and rain to the unrighteous as well as the righteous (5:45). In Matthew, such similarities are not coincidental; they are the heart of the matter.

In the heart of a remarkable passage (11:25–30), Jesus traces his right to act as God to God's act: "All things have been handed over to me by my Father" (verse 27).

The passage is sandwiched between the woes predicted for those who failed to repent and conflicts with Pharisees that led to the plot against Jesus. The passage juxtaposes three types of sayings: (a) prayer thanking the Father for concealing salvation ("these things") from the wise but revealing them to the simple ("infants"); (b) the assertion in verse 27 addressed to the Christian reader; and (c) the invitation to the weary and burdened to find salvation ("rest") by taking up Jesus's word and way (his "yoke").

As the result of God's action, the Son is, so to speak, the Father's alter ego, God's *Doppelgänger*. As "Lord of heaven and earth," the Father remains absolute ground and sovereign, while the Son is "God-as-effect." Far from replacing the Father, the emissary Son replicates God's salvific character and purpose.

Moreover, the Son's knowledge of the Father is exclusive and reciprocal; only the Father knows the Son and vice versa. This reciprocity is the ground of Jesus's soteriological significance, for the Son reveals the Father (anticipating 13:10–17). The invitation to become a disciple of the compassionate Jesus ("gentle and humble in heart," anticipating 12:19–20) implies that the revealed knowledge is essentially moral not cognitive. That is, providing a conceptually precise and accurate understanding of God is not Jesus's central task, but instantiating in his followers the kind of life that reflects the character of the Father.

The whole passage draws on biblical and early Jewish Wisdom theology, without actually using the feminine noun *Sophia*. In this tradition, wisdom had become more than prudent human advice aptly formulated; often she was also imaged as a teacher of the wayward and foolish. Even the structure of 11:25–30 is like that of Proverbs 8: as Jesus's invitation follows the Son's words about himself, so Sophia's invitation in Proverbs 8:22–31 follows her self-proclamation in 8:22–31.

Here Ms. Sophia calls, "learn prudence, acquire intelligence . . . all the words of *my* mouth are righteous." She was God's first act (Proverbs 8:22): "I was beside him, like a master worker" when the Creator "had not yet made earth and fields" (Proverbs 8:26). In the Wisdom of Sirach, Sophia speaks of her way of life on earth as a "yoke" (NRSV "collar") and promises "rest" (6:24,28; also 51:26). Wisdom of Solomon 7:25–27 says she is "a breath of the power of God, and a pure emanation of the glory of the Almighty . . . a reflection of the eternal light . . . she can do all things." According to Enoch 42, she found no home on earth and returned to heaven. Some see this tragic view also in Jesus's lament over Jerusalem in Matthew 23:37: "How often have I desired to gather your children together as a hen gathers her brood under her wings, and you were not willing." Here Jesus appears to be speaking as Sophia herself.

Scholars continue to debate whether, or to what extent, such language is to be treated as poetic personification of an idea (like Lady Luck or Mother Nature) or understood as referring to a discrete heavenly being (a *hypostasis*). The latter view implies the preexistence of Christ, an idea not found unambiguously elsewhere in Matthew but foundational in John. Nor is it clear that holding Jesus to be Wisdom incarnate, as sometimes said, is a necessary component in Matthew's soteriology. In any case, one thing is clear: At no point does Matthew actually assert that Jesus *is* Wisdom, God's agent (or accomplice) in creating the world. In other words, the Evangelist may well have used certain Sophia traits to portray Jesus's role without implying, articulating, or advocating a "Wisdom Christology."

In its own way, Matthew 11:25–30 expresses a "high" Christology. Even so, it barely alludes to topics often deemed essential, and some dots are left unconnected altogether. That said, the fact that Matthew says more about Jesus's message than Romans, while Romans says more about Christ's death as atonement than Matthew, does not imply that one Christology is better, more adequate, more profound than the other. Is Bach better than Brahms?

Matthew, written largely to stabilize and equip a seasoned church bruised by harassment from without and torn by divisions within, does not need to accent the atonement, as does Romans, written four decades before to a new church in order to explain why the resurrection of the crucified Jesus is good news for both Jews and gentiles.

As Matthew nears its end, the Lord's angel orders the Marys at Jesus's empty tomb to tell his disciples to return to Galilee; they will see Jesus *there*. In other words, to see the living, empowering Jesus, they are to return to where it all began. What then was an assignment can today be an invitation: Read Matthew—again!

《 4 》

ROMANS

*Jesus and God's Rectitude**

It is the laying hold of divine rightness that sets wrong men right.

—John Bailey

PAUL, EVER THE audacious apostle, was never more audacious than when he asserted that God's rectitude, God's righteousness, is manifested through the death of Jesus. Should he not have said that the unjust crucifixion of Jesus calls the righteousness of God into question? Why did he not conclude that such a death of such a man manifests God's *un*righteousness? The more we realize that for Paul the righteousness of God was axiomatic, the more astounding is his claim that God's righteousness is actually manifested in the death of Jesus. To see how and why it made sense to Paul, we must first understand why he argues audaciously in Romans, where he speaks most often about the righteousness, or the rectitude, of God.

Ascertaining *how* Paul thought helps us understand what he thought when he wrote Romans, probably the last of his letters. His letters to house churches in Corinth, Galatia, Philippi, and Thessalonika were to be read by new Christians who had heard Paul preach and

---

* This chapter draws on my previous publications that discuss aspects of Paul's thought more fully. In addition to *Paul and His Letters* and the commentary on *Romans*, the collected essays in *Christ's First Theologian* deal with Paul's Jewishness, his ways of thinking, his Letter to the Romans, and his import for today.

teach when he won them to faith in Christ. Those letters focused his thinking on local issues and so never spell out his entire thought. Romans, however, was written for people who, apart from his friends mentioned in the last chapter, had not heard Paul directly, though they had heard about him. But he did not put everything he thought into this letter either. Consequently, what we call the theology of Paul is the result of assembling and ordering his thoughts in a way that makes sense of them all while doing violence to none.

It is impossible, however, to retrace the steps by which he came to the conclusions he reached when writing Romans. While we cannot repeat the steps of Paul's thinking, we can rethink what he thought and wrote. So we begin with the letter and work backward, toward the premises and assumptions on which the arguments rest, and then move forward from there. In proceeding this way, I am not insisting that my inferences are the ones he made. What matters now is whether we find his resulting thought intelligible, coherent, and plausible.

Paul the Theologian

Since we are interested in the Christology that shaped what he said about God's righteousness, the focus is on the way he thought from the starting point, and how this affected the way he thought about Jesus.

The Starting Point
As an unusually zealous Pharisee (Galatians 1:14), he firmly held the theological ideas he inherited and championed. But as a Christian theologian his new starting point was an event. Thus, he was an ex post facto thinker. To think ex post facto is not simply to think after the event has happened, though that is absolutely basic. Above all, to think ex post facto is to think in a certain way *because* of the event, and consistently *in light* of it. Ex post facto thinking is determined by the event. For an ex post facto thinker, the "happenedness" of the event is beyond question, even if it is doubted or denied by others. Because the event is decisive, it requires both new thinking about old thoughts and thinking altogether

new thoughts. Moreover, the ex post facto thinker does not regard the event as a naked fact for which one provides meaning; rather, one discerns and explicates the meaning given "in, with, and under" the event itself.

For Paul, the pivotal event that evoked his ex post facto thinking was the resurrection of the crucified Jesus. In one setting after another, he unfolded the implications of that event by thinking rigorously under its aegis. But he did not start from scratch.

While a Pharisee, Paul had believed that God would resurrect the dead as part of the scenario expected in some forms of Jewish apocalyptic eschatology, according to which God would end the old age and commence the definitively new age. This resurrection, whether of the righteous only or of all the dead, was always to be communal, never of one person only. For the Pharisee Paul, the question was not, Will there be such a thing as resurrection of the dead? but rather, How can anyone claim that resurrection has happened, when it happened only to Jesus? The new age has not arrived; nothing has changed except the foolish people who are announcing publicly that Jesus, and only Jesus, has been resurrected.

How, then did this absurd lie, as it seemed to Paul, become for him the pivotal event whose happenedness was so real that he became a particular kind of ex post facto theologian? This revolution occurred because he became convinced that he had personally experienced the happenedness of Jesus's resurrection. In 1 Corinthians 15 he insists that God had manifested the resurrected Jesus also to him as he had to the original disciples. In Galatians 2 he speaks of this breakthrough as the moment when God "revealed his Son to me." By definition, such an experience is self-authenticating, for the authenticity of God's disclosure cannot be notarized by a neutral party. Nonetheless, that the new age had *not* arrived was as sure as the happenedness of Jesus's resurrection. But how could both be true?

Paul resolved this conundrum by concluding that Jesus's resurrection actually means that the new age has been really inaugurated but will soon be actualized completely. Thus, the happenedness of Jesus's resurrection and the general resurrection remain materially indivisible, but separated in time (as Paul will argue in 1 Corinthians 15:20–28). Accordingly, while Paul can refer to "this age" in Galatians 1:4, he never speaks of "the age to come," because for him it is now inaugurated. While it is likely that the first Jewish believers also thought that Jesus's resurrection signaled the intrusion of the new age, it was Paul's rigorous and relentless ex post facto thinking that exploited so audaciously the logical consequences of the Easter event.

Understanding Paul's thought therefore requires thinking with him, and that entails looking at everything through the lens of Jesus's resurrection as *he* understood it. And that might require us to set aside, at least for the moment, both our own problem with the very idea of resurrection and all explanations of it that emphasize what happened to the disciples and ignore whatever happened to Jesus. What matters just now is not whether Paul was right, but whether we can set aside our own views in order to understand Paul's. Otherwise, we will not understand him at all.

The Two-Age Logic

How pervasively the two-age schema, the framework for Paul's ex post facto thinking, affected the way he thought becomes evident when we look at *two* aspects of his thought. The *first* concerns the logic of the two-age schema itself. By definition, its dualistic view of history expresses a negative judgment on the past and present. Two-age thinking judges the historical reality in light of what is expected. Past and present are what Paul calls "the present evil age" (Galatians 1:4). The present is not evil because of Rome's hegemony is oppressive, but because human existence in history has come under the control of malign powers. Consequently, the transition from the present age to the age to come is not a matter of reform but of release from the powers that have usurped God's rightful place as ruler of the created order. Whereas probably every generation in the West since the Enlightenment has seen itself as the apex of ceaseless, though repeatedly interrupted, progress toward some telos of history, the two-age schema assumes that the definitive telos will occur only when God ends "this age" and brings on "the age to come," which Paul calls "new creation." While he never describes this transition, we may infer that for him the new creation will not replace heaven and earth with a new universe altogether, as in Revelation 21, but will transform creation by releasing it from bondage to the powers and from the inevitability of death, the sign of their reign.

The discontinuity between the two ages is reflected in three features of Paul's theological thinking: first, he too devalues the present from the standpoint of the future when, for example, he tells the Romans, "I consider that the sufferings of this present time are not worth comparing with the glory about to be revealed to us." Indeed, "the whole creation has been groaning in labor pains until now," eagerly awaiting the birth of the new age, just as Christians are groaning for the "redemption" of their bodies from death and decay (8:18–23). Second, since he understands the present in light of the future, his thought moves from solution to plight, as Ed Sanders insisted. It is the character of salvation that discloses the real nature of sin; it is the presence of the Spirit that reveals the power of the flesh. And third, given the deep discontinuity between the new age and the present, Paul's thought moves in contrasts, like bondage and freedom, death and life, Spirit and flesh.

The *second* impact of two-age thinking appears in his ability to think holistically. The two-age schema has little interest in making distinctions within this age; what matters are the characteristics that determine and characterize this age as a whole and so mark it off radically from the age to come. For example, even though the Book of Daniel symbolizes the sequence of empires as a series of animals, what really matters is not their individual traits but their shared bestial character when compared with the humanoid Son of Man kingdom.

So too, Paul shows no interest in making distinctions within the realities that he discusses. When discussing the law, he ignores the difference between cultic and moral law, between apodictic law ("thou shalt") and case law ("if this happens, then do that"). Nor does he show interest in distinguishing deliberate, willful disobedience from accidental transgression, or between grosser and lesser sins. What matters is Sin, not sins; the Law, not particular laws. His thinking reaches for that quality in law or sin that determines its true character because that determines how it impinges on the self. Definitions based on essences play no role in his thought, whether he is discussing desire, flesh, Spirit, death, or even resurrection.

Paul's Thinking About Jesus

It is Paul's holistic thinking that largely accounts for the way he thinks about Jesus. Because Paul's holistic thinking has not been grasped adequately, his way of referring to Jesus has not been grasped properly either. His few references to Jesus's words, coupled with his many references to Christ, have been an enigma that defies an historical explanation, one that appeals to his circumstances. Often we assume that he should have referred to Jesus the way we would. To be concrete, Paul twice refers to "Abba" as the distinguishing feature of Christian prayer (Romans 8:15; Galatians 4:6), but why does he not remind the readers that Jesus too addressed God this way? Likewise, why does Paul's whole discussion of the law, including freedom from the law, never mention Jesus's words or deeds as either the defining precedent or final norm?

Historical explanations are usually unconvincing. For instance, if one argues that Paul probably did not know the relevant stories and sayings of Jesus, one simply converts Paul's silence into evidence of his ignorance. Somewhat more persuasive is the claim that where Paul's point resembles what the Gospels tell us Jesus did or said, he was alluding to Jesus without actually mentioning him. This is possible. But normally an author makes an allusion when he can assume that the readers will recognize it; otherwise, it is lost. So if we say that Paul was alluding to Jesus, we must assume that he counted on his readers' knowledge of the still unwritten Jesus traditions in order to register the allusions, and that in turn requires us to explain how Paul's new Christians came to know the traditions so well. One can, of course, argue plausibly that Paul himself had conveyed those traditions when he instructed his converts in Corinth, Galatia, Philippi, and Thessalonika. But that would not account for the alleged allusions in the letter to his Roman readers who had not yet heard him. In short, we do not have enough information about the collection and circulation of the Jesus traditions in the first decades of Christianity to develop a convincing historical explanation of what we find about Jesus in Paul's letters. But even if that were possible, it would still miss the central point—that it is precisely Paul's holistic ex post facto thinking within the framework of the two-age schema that accounts *theologically* for the way Paul wrote about Jesus.

Since Paul thinks ex post facto from the happenedness of Jesus's resurrection and the whole Jesus event, the new creation did not break into the present age when Jesus healed the sick or taught what we find in the Sermon on the Mount, even if Paul knew those traditions. Just as Paul did not understand the character of this age by examining its various particular traits or by blaming them on certain persons or groups but by discerning its defining character as a whole, so he found the significance of the Jesus event in its overall character, in Jesus's determinative obedience, not in the details of his mission. Had Paul emphasized Jesus's teachings, he would have been Jesus's disciple—a word absent from Paul's letters. Instead, he is Christ's emissary, an apostle. For Paul, one is no more saved from "this evil age" by obeying Jesus than one is saved from it by obeying Moses. Healing the human condition requires something other, but not less than obedience. What makes Jesus definitive is not the superiority of his teaching compared with Moses (or anybody else), but his resurrection, the inauguration of the new age. Moses belongs to the old age. In short, because Paul thought holistically about the entire Jesus event in light of the resurrection, he did not arrive in Philippi or Corinth with the news about a better teacher, a superior exegete, a more effective miracle worker, a more holy more Spirit-filled man, or the founder of a more inclusive movement. Jesus's resurrection precluded all such comparative judgments. "Better" is not part of Paul's Christological vocabulary, as it will be for Hebrews.

But the resurrection did not occur to any dead person, but precisely to Jesus and only to Jesus the crucified. Because for Paul a righteous God does not act arbitrarily or impulsively, by resurrecting Jesus, God vindicated the Jesus event as a whole, and that implies that God validated Jesus's defining characteristic—obedience. Consequently, the character of the new age coheres with the character of the Jesus event, which in turn is consonant with the character of God.

The Anthropological/Soteriological Correlate

This last observation brings us to the threshold of Paul's Christology to its theological correlate (Jesus's relation to God) and its anthropological/soteriological correlate (the human plight and its resolution through the Jesus event). In Romans there are two analyses of the human plight, the first in chapters 1–4, the second in chapters 5–8, and it is with the latter that we begin.

The Rhetorical Strategy

But first, we see something that needs to be explained. If Paul's thought moved from solution to plight, why does he first expound the human plight (from 1:18–3:20) before discussing the solution? The reason is not obscure: Paul is not recording the flow of his thoughts during his conversion; rather, he is ordering them in a way designed to persuade the readers to agree with him so that—among other things—they will support his future mission in Spain which he expects to launch after coming to Rome. His analysis of the human plight begins with a remarkable assertion about the gospel: "It is the power of God for salvation for *everyone* who believes, for the Jew first and also for the Greek, for in it God's righteousness is being revealed" (1:16–17) He does not say that the gospel is about God's power, but that it is God's power, God's effective means of salvation because it manifests God's righteousness. Right from the start, it is clear that in Romans God's righteousness,

God's rectitude, is a salvific event for *all* who entrust themselves to this news about God. This implies that there is one salvation for everyone, whether one is a member of the chosen people who have the law, or a gentile without it. Thus, the letter to Roman believers is the first Christian theology of mission, especially to gentiles. To persuade his readers, Paul begins with the need for this mission.

Because Paul writes to persuade people he has not yet met and whom he has not yet taught, his two-age thinking is not always explicit but often remains implicit. Only at the beginning of his exhortation does he actually allude to the two ages. There he urges the readers not to be "conformed to this age" but rather to be transformed by the renewal of their minds (12:2). Nonetheless, the influence of the two-age schema is apparent throughout and is especially evident in chapter 5, where Christ inaugurates the new age antidote to the old age that began with Adam. Two-age thinking is present also in chapter 8, where Paul writes of the redemption of all creation, as he must if Jesus's resurrection inaugurated the age to come, for by definition, the new age is not another phase in Roman or Jewish history but the alternative to all history since Adam. In chapter 8 Paul interprets God's curse on the ground that followed Adam's disobedience and says that God subjected creation to *douleia tes phthonos*, which NRSV renders as "bondage to decay" but REB renders more colorfully as "shackles of mortality." The point is that because of Adam, creation itself was changed; now every living thing is transitory, subject to inevitable death. Mortality has become the hallmark of creation in this age.

Also present is the holistic thinking that flows from the two-age schema. In chapter 5 Paul writes that "sin entered the world through one man, and death came through sin, and in this way sin spread to all men inasmuch as all sinned" (5:1). Paul's holistic thinking is apparent here because he does not differentiate between kinds or degrees of sin; what matters is that sin as such is the despoiler of all creation as the handiwork of God. Here all sin, by definition, is mortal sin, for as Paul says later, "the wages of sin is death"—and the wages are always paid. In fact, because of Paul's holistic thinking, the wages of Adam are paid even to plants and animals, not only to Adam's human offspring. So, then, when Paul writes disparagingly of "this age" he is not engaging in a bit of cultural criticism. He is grasping the ecology of creation's fallenness as a whole.

Accordingly, in chapter 8, holistic thinking appears in the connection between the redemption of the believer and the redemption of creation: because the believer's body is part of creation, the redemption of the body is inseparable from the redemption of all creation from its "shackles of mortality." Just as Paul's discussion of the law ignores the differences between kinds of law, so here his holistic thinking lets him ignore the differences between various kinds of living beings because his eye is on what determines the plight of creation as a whole.

Further, Paul's holistic thinking about Adam solves a problem created by holistic thinking's disregard of distinctions within entities. This feature of holistic thinking, however, conflicts with the one distinction within humanity that for Paul is not triviable—the distinction between Jew and gentile. How, then, does Paul deal with this apparent inconsistency? Somehow, he must show that "all are under sin" (3:9), that "there is no distinction, since all have sinned" (3:23), although only the Jew has the law which identifies sin. In order to make Jew and gentile equally guilty, Paul argues that when the gentile who does not have the law by nature (i.e., by ethnic identity), nonetheless does what the law requires, the gentile actually does follow law—the law written on the heart—and the phenomenon of conscience shows it. By this strategy, Paul tries to level the playing field. Nonetheless, can this argument succeed? Not by itself, for it still assumes the difference between Jew and gentile, traceable to the election of Abraham and solidified in the law of Moses—a difference that occurred *within* history. The problem requires a solution that is more fundamental. The logical tension between the holistic disregard of distinctions within humanity and the Jew–gentile distinction is resolved when Paul traces the human situation to Adam's disobedience at the outset of history. Whereas Abraham and Moses divide humanity, Adam unites it. Adam's originating disobedience provides a holistic understanding of the undifferentiated human situation. In short, Jews are as Adamic as gentiles, and just as destined for death.

The Dilemma and the Condition

Paul's discussion of Adam and Christ in chapter 5 is important for another reason: It signals a turn in his treatment of the entire anthropological/soteriological correlate in the Christology of Romans. Whereas the discussion in the first four chapters (especially the first three) interpreted the human situation as the *dilemma* of being guilty of disobedience before God's impartial judgment, the turn to Adam initiates a discussion of the human plight as a *condition*: one's very existence is distorted and doomed by bondage to mortality and sin. Whereas in chapters 1–3 Paul regards sin as transgression of God's will, and sins as deeds for which one is accountable, in chapters 5–8 his holistic thinking leads him to probe more deeply. Here sin is much more than the doer's wrong deed resulting in a wrong relation to the impartial righteous God; here sin is an enslaving power. Here sin is the doer, enslaving the self (6:6), exercising its malign power through the body's desires (6:12), having taken up residence in the self. Now sin is proactive, preventing one from doing the intended good, and provoking one to do the evil not intended (7:19). Likewise, in chapters 6–8, death is more than the inevitable end of life; here one is dead before dying, for death is a power that rules the living (5:17), for as the inevitable consequence of sin, it is an inner tyrant.

The difference between the dilemma and the condition is important. The dilemma results from sin as disobedience that puts one in a wrong relation to God's impartial judgment; that dilemma is resolved when the relation to God is made right (which is what justification means). On the other hand, since the condition is a damaged state of existence shared with every living being, everyone is trapped and cannot escape by deciding to emigrate because the condition itself, acting as an enslaving power, functions as a field of force that prevents one from doing what one wants to do, including wanting to leave the distorted state of being. No one, no matter how determined or self-disciplined, is powerful enough to escape the power of the condition, this age, the unavoidable legacy of Adam.

Since the cure must fit the disease, the solution to being caught in the condition is being liberated from it—a liberation that occurs when one enters a totally different condition, a new field of force, a mode of existence completely free from the power of sin and death; this new field of force is Christ.

Accordingly, Paul points out that Christ, "being raised from the dead, will never die again; death no longer has dominion over him" (6:9). Therefore, whoever participates in Christ shares in his victory over sin and death, the event that inaugurated the new age. Thus, participating in Christ inaugurates the saving alternative to participating in Adam. Because Christ's resurrection inaugurated this new mode of existence but did not bring it about fully, living now according to the new life in Christ is the "already" that anticipates what is "not yet" complete, the full transformation of the current state of existence when all creation will be liberated. In other words, participation in Christ conveys ex post facto salvation as anticipation.

The logic of participation, the antidote to the human condition, differs from the logic of rectification developed in chapters 1–4, concerned with the dilemma of being wrongly related to God the impartial judge whose will is expressed in the law. This wrongness is not an error that can be overlooked or outgrown by conscientious effort, for it is radical and ubiquitous.

Paul's interpretation of the dilemma begins at 1:18, where he declares that God's wrath is "against all ungodliness and wickedness [or injustice, *adikia*] of persons who by *adikia* suppress the truth." And as the interpretation ends, Paul claims that everyone, "both Jews and Greeks, is *under* sin" (3:9)—a phrase that links the human dilemma to the human condition as subservience. To support the radicality and universality of this plight, Paul adduces a string of biblical quotations, the first of which declares, "There is no one who is righteous, not even one." The other quotations assert that no one understands or seeks God, or shows kindness; instead, they lie, kill, and destroy. Later Paul will characterize this breakdown of rightness as enmity with God (5:10). When he concludes his analysis, he uses words from Psalm 143 to declare, "all flesh will not be declared right [or made right, rectified] on the basis of deeds prescribed by the law, for through the law comes knowledge of sin" (3:20). Wrongly related persons cannot rectify themselves by relying on the very law that shows just how wrong they are. Only God can make right everything that has gone wrong, and this rectification occurs apart from the law. Indeed, it must.

And in this part of Romans, that rectification is exactly what the inauguration of the new age means ex post facto the Jesus event. That is why the news about that event discloses God's own rightness, God's own righteousness. Indeed, the news itself is God's power to save everyone who believes the announcement of what God has done in that event. Explaining God's role in that event is the task of the theological correlate.

The Theological Correlate in Romans

The theological correlate appears in the opening sentence of Romans, where Paul says who he is in relation to Christ (his slave) and who Christ is in relation to God: the promised Son of God who from human perspective became David's descendant (i.e., Son of David), and who in terms of the "Spirit of holiness" was then designated Son of God with power by his resurrection. Despite some scholars' denials, here the preexisting Son became the Davidic Messiah—a status Paul acknowledges (also 9:5) but does not emphasize. Moreover, Paul alludes to the preexistent Son also in 8:3, where he writes, "What the law could not do . . . God has done: By sending his own Son in the likeness of our sinful nature and to deal with sin, he passed judgment against sin within that very nature" (as REB puts it). That the preexistent Son was sent into the human plight Paul asserts also in Galatians 4:4: "God sent his Son, born of a woman, born under the law in order to redeem those under the law." The combination of preexistence, existence, and postexistence gives the Christ event a U-shape, which appears also in the Christological hymn in Philippians 2. While Paul says little about the preexistence of the Son (see 1 Corinthians 8:6; 10:3), his whole Christology assumes it, and his soteriology simply will not "work" without it.

For the theme of Jesus's relation to the righteousness of God, the key passage is 3:21–26, where Paul announces that God's righteousness, God's rectitude, is manifested apart from the law. Douglas Campbell has clarified this long complex sentence by identifying a parenthesis within it; when this parenthesis is ignored, the rhetorical structure of the passage emerges clearly. Now we can see that Paul interprets God's rectitude apart from the law in two steps: in the first he uses three parallel statements that specify the *means* by which God's rectitude was disclosed, each beginning with the same Greek word, *dia* (through), and each referring to Jesus's death; in the second, he uses three parallel phrases to state the *goal* or result of this disclosure.

Of the three phrases, the second says that God put forward Christ as the *hilasterion*. We need not decide whether it means place of atonement, sacrifice for sins, or expiation; what matters here is seeing that this is cultic language about the power of blood sacrifice to remove sin and so restore a right relation to God. What makes this assertion significant is the claim that God acted here, precisely in Jesus's death. Since human sacrifice had long been condemned in Scripture, such an act was itself "apart from the law," indeed, contrary to it. To account for this astounding assertion, commentators frequently refer to 4 Maccabees 17, which says that God reckoned the death of the martyrs as *hilasterion* for the nation. There God's reckoning was an ex post facto reward for their life-giving loyalty to the law, but in our passage the blood sacrifice of Jesus's death was the result of God's initiative. What Paul says here agrees with what he will say in 5:8, that God "demonstrates *his* love for us in that while we were still sinners *Christ* [i.e., not martyrs] died for us." Here too, without preexistence, God's providing Jesus as the *hilasterion* would be evidence of God's arbitrary act of unrighteousness, an act that some have condemned as child abuse. But this view misses the point profoundly because Paul assumes—as people did generally—that the son represents the father. Consequently, providing the preexistent Son as the *hilasterion* actually expresses the self-involvement of God in Jesus's death.

The two other *dia* statements explain Jesus's death as the means by which God's rectitude was manifested. The first says simply that it occurred *dia pisteos Iesou Christou*, namely "through the faithfulness of Jesus Christ" (not "through faith in Christ"). The second explains the *hilasterion* as occurring *dia tos pisteos en to autou haimati*, "through faithfulness actualized in his blood." Both of these statements are consistent with what Paul will say later in connection with Adam and Christ: "For just as by one man's disobedience, the many were made sinners, so by one man's obedience the many will be made righteous" (5:19).

In the last of the three statements of the goal or result of God's action, Paul says that God demonstrated "that he himself is righteous and rectifies *ton ek pisteos* of Jesus," which should be translated as "the person who lives by the faithfulness of Jesus," not "the person who has faith in Jesus," though one would not live by the faithfulness of Jesus if one did not also entrust oneself to him.

The whole paragraph is about what God has done that showed his rectitude apart from the law; it is not about what human faith can do. That is, God shows his rectitude precisely in rectifying the person who lives on the basis of the faithfulness of Jesus, actualized in his death. Because the whole event occurred by God's initiative and not in response to human achievement prescribed by the law, God's rectitude rectifies apart from the law. That is why Paul can refer to God in the next chapter as the one "who rectifies the ungodly." The gods who operate according to law rectify the godly.

Strange as Paul's reasoning may seem, it begins to make sense when we dare to think boldly with him—that is, to think ex post facto within the framework of the two ages. To summarize: (a) God resurrected Jesus. His resurrection inaugurated the new age, the new creation. By definition, the new creation rectifies all that has gone wrong since Adam. Therefore, in resurrecting Jesus, God begins rectifying everyone and everything; (b) because God is not arbitrary or whimsical but self-consistent (i.e., rightly related to the norm of God's own self), rectification reveals the character of God, for what God does shows who God is. Since rectification is grounded only in God's character, rectification occurs apart from the law; (c) Paul would not have said such things apart from the event of Jesus, capped by the cross and validated by resurrection. Because Jesus is the Son of God, his faithfulness into death manifests the faithfulness of God to creation; (d) God is never more righteous, God's rectitude is never more clear, than in rectifying the person who lives by the faithfulness of Jesus into his death. That is, God comes through as God in rectifying the ungodly.

In a sense, Romans is an extended commentary on what Paul had written to the Corinthians: "in Christ God was reconciling the world to himself, not counting their trespasses against them," followed a few lines later with "for our sake he made him [Christ] to be sin who knew no sin, so that in him we might become the righteousness of God"—that is, that we might become the rectifying rectitude of God actualized (2 Corinthians 5:19, 21). Like the resurrection of the crucified Jesus, so also the rectification of the ungodly apart from the law manifests the righteousness of God.

❧ 5 ❧

JOHN

Jesus and the Exegesis of God

Probably no writing of the New Testament is explained more wrongly than the Gospel of John.

—William Wrede

How difficult is it not to see John as the kind of thinker one would like to be.

—John Ashton

"HE IS DIFFICULT only if you try to understand him." This verdict about the poet G. Manley Hopkins applies also to this Gospel. Of the four Gospels, it is the easiest to read but the hardest to understand, and explain historically.

This Gospel's Challenges

John is an exasperating account of an exasperating figure. Looking briefly at its probable matrix, its unusual mode of narration, and its arresting mind can disclose why its readers—devotees included—often find it as frustrating as inspiring.

Its Elusive Setting

Ascertaining the various factors that prompted the creation of this Gospel, and shaped its content, is made more difficult if the three anonymous "Letters of John" are taken into account as well.[1] Whether all the data *can* be connected into a coherent, though incomplete, picture is not self-evident. But even a sketch of John's readers is helpful in understanding the Gospel written for them.

The Johannine community (or communities) was plagued by intense controversies, including a power struggle between the elder who wrote 3 John and an otherwise unknown Diotrephes, said to "put himself first," and not to acknowledge "our authority." He also spreads "false charges against us," refuses hospitality to the elder's group, and expels those who offer it anyway. In 2 John, however, the church is told not to welcome the "many deceivers" who did not confess "that Jesus Christ has come in the flesh"; such a deceiver is nothing less than the antichrist (verse 7). In 1 John this label is applied to a breakaway group (2:18–19) with a deceitful Christology (2:22–27; 4:3. Were they Diotrephes's followers?). So 1 John emphasizes continuity with the received truth: "Let what you heard from the beginning abide in you" (2:24).

Though the Gospel mentions none of these controversies explicitly, it appears to allude to them allegorically. Its Jesus also prays for the church's unity (17:11), and its prologue declares that "flesh" is exactly what the Word "became."

The Gospel's last chapter implies that the community was polarized by other issues as well. On the one hand, it reflects an odd rivalry between Peter and an anonymous "disciple whom Jesus loved," that is, between their followers.[2] Only in John do we read of the beloved disciple, not identified as the son of the Galilean fisherman, Zebedee (Mark 1:19–20).

At the Last Supper, Peter asks the beloved disciple "reclining next to Jesus" to ask Jesus to identify the betrayer (13:23–25). The beloved one might be "the other disciple" who, being known to the high priest, facilitated Peter's admission to the high priest's courtyard where Peter denied knowing Jesus (18:15–18). On Easter morning he outran Peter, reached and entered the empty tomb first, and "believed" before Peter and Mary Magdalene (20:1–18). At Jesus's appearance to his (seven!) disciples in

Galilee, it is the beloved disciple who tells Peter that the figure on the shore is the Lord (21:7). A bit later, Peter confessed his love for Jesus. Jesus, having committed the church to Peter's care (21:15–17), rebuked Peter for wanting to know whether the beloved disciple's death would be like his own (21:18–23). Curiously, the narrator corrects a rumor that the beloved disciple would not die at all (21:23).

On the other hand, 21:24 not only asserts that the beloved disciple testifies to these things and has written them but also declares, "We know that his teaching is true." This suggests theological controversy as well. John 19:35 insists that blood and water really did flow from Jesus's spear-pierced side because the beloved disciple saw it. Is it accidental that all references to the beloved disciple occur in the passages not paralleled in the other Gospels?[3]

The Gospel and Johannine Epistles provide enough data to generate "explanations" but not enough to build a construction of the past that convinces most scholars for long. The date and place of John's composition remain unknown. The Gospel may contain earlier Christian writings and traditions that sometimes seem to be in tension with other parts. If so, it would be misleading to speak of the "author." Rather, the Gospel is "layered" with diverse Johannine material, assembled and edited in ways hard to recover correctly.[4]

Remarkably, neither John 21 nor the Johannine Epistles mention Jesus's controversies with "the Jews" that permeate John 5–12. The content of the disputes, however, reflects the Christological issues that later separated Christians and Jews, especially Jesus's unique relationship to God. What the narrator retrojects into Jesus's time (in 9:22 and 12:42), Jesus himself predicts in 16:2, "They will put you out of synagogues. Indeed, the time will come when those who kill you will think that by doing so they are offering worship to God."[5]

Finally, a word about "the Fourth Gospel." Convinced that the Gospel was not written by the disciple John, scholars call it "The Fourth Gospel" instead—and thereby often load the dice of interpretation unwittingly. "The Fourth Gospel" means but one thing: It now occupies the fourth position in the New Testament. This implies nothing whatever about John's place in early Christianity. No one knows which Gospel was the fourth to be written. Nor does "fourth" imply anything about the character of John's content; that is, given the search for reliable historical information about Jesus, John's theology-laden account has often been devalued as "unhistorical." On the other hand, as the *fourth* gospel, John has also been valued as the apex of New Testament theology's development toward a late first/early second century "high" Christology—as if early Christian thought moved on a conceptual escalator to the fourth floor. To avoid tacitly perpetuating this historical illusion, this book discusses John's Christology third, not fourth.

John's Fascinating Mode

As used here, "mode" is more than style and other than genre. It refers to the particular manner in which the story of Jesus is told. The Gospel's manner accords with what 1 John boldly asserts: "We declare . . . what we have heard, what we have seen with our eyes . . . concerning the word of life—this life was revealed and we have seen it and testify (*martyroumen*) to it" (1 John 1:1–2, also 4:14 and 5:9–12). The Gospel's final two verses also insist that "we know that his [the beloved disciple's] testimony (martyria) is true." The location of this comment implies that it pertains to the whole preceding narrative.[6]

In bearing witness/testifying, one vouches for the truth one has experienced. Without denigrating proper cognition, witnessing is a deeply personal act. It does not, however, occur for the speaker's/writer's benefit but for the hearer's/reader's. According to 20:30–31, the purpose of this witness is not self-expression (though this happens as well) but confirmation or persuasion of others.

In John's testimonial narrative, the true significance of Jesus is not derived only from the reader's "meaningful" interpretation of him; one is also confronted by an already-interpreted, vouched-for Jesus who interprets the reader.

Accordingly, John's narrative often blurs the distinction between past and present, between what was true then and what is still true as in Jesus's disputes with "the Jews" noted above. Such blurring of time makes it difficult to know where Jesus's words to Nicodemus in John 3 end and where his words to readers begin.[7]

This seamlessness between what Jesus said then and what he says now draws readers of the Gospel into the narrative, so they can be confronted by the same Jesus that confronted characters *in* the narrative. In other words, through John's witness mode the readers encounter the is-ness of the Jesus who was.[8]

That the whole Gospel is to be read as the believers' witness to the salvific truth of Jesus is signaled also at the outset—in the prologue's assertions "*We have seen* his glory" and "from his fullness *we have all received*" (1:14, 18). This "we" appears again, in the middle of Jesus's own testimony to Nicodemus: "*We* speak of what *we know* and testify to what *we have seen*" (3:11). In this narrative, events once seen and words once heard by few are presented simultaneously as testimony to their continuing salvific meaning to everyone.

"Seeing," in fact, is central in everything reported in the latter part of John's opening chapter (see 1:19, 29, 35, 39, 46–50), capped by Jesus's promises to Nathaniel: "You will see greater things than these," viz, "You will see heaven opened and the angels of God ascending and descending upon the Son of Man" (verse 51, alluding to the patriarch Jacob's dream, Genesis 28:2–12).[9]

But what is there to see, to observe, in this man from Nazareth, from which nothing good is expected (1:46)? Indeed, what Jesus said to "the Jews" at the end of a controversy can also be taken as the narrator's hermeneutical counsel to the readers: "Do not judge *by* appearances (*kat' opsin*) but with right judgment" (7:24). That is, the apparent, the obvious, the phenomenal that is visible to anyone, is not to be the criterion by which one determines what is really going on in the Jesus event.

The counsel does not, however, disparage the apparent, for the narrator provides information—explanations and translations (such as 4:9 and 1:41, respectively) and sundry details—that anchor the account in real time and place.[10] As testimony to the truth about Jesus, John challenges its readers to a venturous kind of "seeing," one that penetrates the surface (the correct fact) in order to grasp what is really happening religiously (i.e., in relation to God) *in* the observable event. Without this perceptive "seeing," at best Jesus's deeds are religiously "interesting," and usually controversial.

Although John often refers to the many "signs" (*semei*) that Jesus did (e.g., 2:23, 3:2, 6:2, 11:47, 12:37), it highlights seven miracles, none of them exorcisms:

2:1–11	turning water into wine
4:46–54	healing a royal official's son
5:2–18	healing paralysis on sabbath
6:2–14	feeding a crowd
6:16–21	walking on the lake
9:1–41	healing a lifelong blindness
11:1–44	restoring Lazarus to life

These miracles always *show* but never *establish* the truth about Jesus (he refuses to "do" a legitimating sign). To the perceptive eye, their beneficent character points beyond their immediate, apparent, particular effect; the act is translucent enough to imply Jesus's significance for the human condition. As signs, both the deeds done and the stories telling them signal truth that needs to be discerned. For John, these miracles happened. Without the act, there is no "sign." The story is not a literary precipitate of an idea, an allegory, but a pointer to the truth *in* the reported deed. Those who see only the deed (or only read of it as information) do not realize that what they are looking at *is* a sign, and so miss the point of what they do see and of their seeing it.

Whereas *semeia* tells readers how to approach the stories of Jesus's miracles, the word Jesus himself uses to interpret his mission is *ergon*, "work." While "sign" has in view a particular act, "work" refers comprehensively to the significance of Jesus's activity, especially in relation to God's own activity. "Work" is Jesus's testimony word for his vocation. The witness terminology of the narrator and of Jesus is complementary. While every sign is a work, a work need not be a sign (a miracle), for to Jesus's work belong his teachings as well.

According to 4:34, Jesus's task is to "complete" (*teleioso*) God's work, specified at 6:29: "This is the work of God, that you believe in him whom he has sent." In 9:4 he says, "We must work the works of him who sent me"; in 10:25 he asserts, "the works that I do in my Father's name testify to me." Reflecting on his mission, he says he glorified God by "completing" (*teleiosas*) the work God gave him (17:4). On the cross, he declared triumphantly, *tetelestai* ("it is completed").

Though Jesus calls himself a "worker" (*ergates*), "works" frequently refers to the diverse means by which he does God's one work, and so actualizes his identity as the Son of the working Father (see 5:17). So, too, the works of the world (7:7), as of the disciples (14:12), actualize who/what the doers really are.

In short, in John, Jesus's "signs" instantiate Christology's anthropological/soteriological correlate, and his "works" express its *theo*logical correlate.

Like the significance of Jesus's deeds, the truth of his words is not obvious; discerning it entails understanding what is really meant by what is actually said. Thus Jesus, having disrupted commerce in the temple precinct, responds to a request for a legitimating "sign" with a riddle: "Destroy this temple, and in three days I will raise it up." Taken literally, this is ridiculous. The narrator, however, explains what "temple" really means and so alerts the reader to Jesus's peculiar use of language in the rest of the account (2:13–21).

His vocabulary, like the narrator's, is free of abstractions and the terminology of philosophy like *hypostasis* (substance) or *apaugasma* (radiation), both important in the Letter to the Hebrews. Instead, Jesus uses simple words for ordinary things (e.g., bread, gate, house, light, water) to assert complex ideas—not to talk down to his cognitive inferiors. Rather, by using simple words with multiple meanings, he discloses whether his hearers get the point, as in the riddle just noted. Thus, he says figuratively that Nicodemus must be born *anothen* (from above), but the sage hears it literally as "over again" (from the mother's womb), and is baffled by this oxymoron.

From John's angle, such misunderstandings are neither unforeseen consequences of good intentions nor symptoms of Jesus's unfortunate failure to communicate. Rather, they are inevitable when the Logos, enfleshed as an autodidact (7:15), confronts people who "loved darkness rather than light because their deeds were evil" (3:19). In fact, it was foretold in Isaiah 6, thus implying God's will (John 12:37–40). Nonetheless, Jesus's own mission does the "work" of God.

John's Jesus differs significantly from Matthew's. What is unusual in Matthew—Jesus's self-proclamation in Matthew 11:25–27— dominates Jesus's teaching in John. Conversely, the theme of his message in Matthew—the kingdom of God—is mentioned only once in John (3:3), and the call to repentance is absent altogether. John's Jesus experiences neither temptation in the wilderness nor agony in the Garden. Instead of criticizing the Pharisees' use of oral tradition in their interpretation of Scripture, as in Matthew 15:1–20, he affirms that he is the one Moses wrote about (5:46).

What really distinguishes John's Jesus from Matthew's is neither Davidic descent nor virgin birth, but incarnation. As a result, Matthew and John talk about the same *man* Jesus, not about the same *person*. John's Jesus speaks and acts differently because he is "other." This otherness never eclipses Jesus's vulnerability to fatigue, thirst, hunger, sorrow, and momentary anguish (see 4:6–7, 19:28, 4:31–33, 11:35–36, and 12:27, respectively). Here may lie the most significant challenge in the study of John's Christology: to detect and delineate the logic of Christology embedded in a narrative of this sui generis person.

Remarkable details attest Jesus's otherness. Though distant, he recognizes Nathaniel's moral excellence (1:47) and also heals a boy (4:46). Having walked on the storm-tossed lake, the disciples' boat reached land "immediately" (6:16–21). Even the authorities who arrested him stepped back and "fell to the ground" because they sensed the awesome numinous "other" when he identified himself by using God's self-disclosure to Moses: "I am" (18:6).

Even more remarkable is 2:23–25: Though many saw his "signs" and became believers, Jesus "would not entrust himself to them, because he knew all people and needed no one to testify about anyone; for he himself knew what was in everyone." Accordingly, the account of his public activity (chapters 1–12) never shows him affirming anyone.

Thus, when Nicodemus asks for an explanation of the new birth, Jesus replies not with an encouraging word but with an ad hominem rebuke, "Are you a teacher of Israel, and you do not understand these things?" (3:2–10). Even more severe is his response to Simon Peter's confession, "We have come to believe and know that you are the Holy One of God" (6:66–70). Instead of responding with a beatitude (as in Matthew 16:17) Jesus says, "Did I not choose you, the 12? Yet one of you is a devil." Martha's exemplary confession (11:27) gets no response at all. When the crowd began to regard Jesus as the expected prophet because he had miraculously fed them, he accuses them, "You are looking for me not because you saw signs, but because you ate your fill of the loaves" (6:26).

The figure portrayed in chapters 1–12 differs significantly from the Jesus shown in chapters 13–17. In the former he is aggressive and adversarial; in the latter, when he is alone with "his own," he is affirmative and pastoral, showing concern for their well-being.[11]

Yet even at the intimate private Supper, Jesus does not simply affirm, or accept at face value, the disciples' avowals of fidelity. To Simon Peter's pledge to die for Jesus, he responds by predicting the disciple's triple denial (13:36–38). Philip's request, "Lord, show us the *Father*, and we will be satisfied," gets a Christological rebuke (recalling Nicodemus, see above). "Have I been with you all this time . . . and you still do not know *me*?" (14:8). When the disciples claim that they believe that he came from God, he taunts them, "Do you *now* believe? You will be scattered [and] . . . leave me alone" (16:29–32).

This "otherness," John implies, is more than an unusual, irritating aspect of Jesus's personality. It belongs to the heart of John's Christology and must be understood as such. That is, John assumes that only by being consistently and inherently "other" can Jesus from Nazareth be "the savior of the world" (4:42).

What probably made this bold Christology plausible in its first matrix was its particular mindset, a way of thinking. That mentality deserves brief comment before we examine the correlates of John's Christology.

The Johannine Mind

To begin with, the Johannine mindset accounts for the way the Gospel speaks of "*flesh*." Basic is what Jesus says to Nicodemus: "What is born of flesh is flesh, and what is born of Spirit is spirit" (3:6). Each reality reproduces only its own kind; neither generates a mutation. The difference between them is radical, a given; it is simply "the way things are." It is not contingent on circumstances; it is structural. In John, it is always a matter of either/or, never both/and, or partly this/partly that. There is no associate membership in the Johannine community, and secret adherents are disdained as fearful (12:42–43).[12] Jesus also says "It is the Spirit that gives life; the flesh is useless" (6:63).

Flesh is not inherently evil, however. Nor does the Gospel blame flesh for the human condition. Still, "flesh" is not a neutral, value-free synonym for the body, either. It is a value-laden term that calls attention to the inability of the phenomenal and the merely physical to generate eternal life. The Johannine mind does not equate contrast with conflict. It can therefore think dualistically without assuming or advocating dual*ism*. Avoiding dualism also enables Jesus to say that "those who eat my flesh abide in me and I in them" (6:56). That is, partakers of the eucharist do not take into themselves the preexistent Word, but the Word enfleshed.

In addition, the Johannine mind emphasizes *knowing*. John therefore regards knowing God and Christ rightly as the signature of salvation, and knowing them wrongly as the mark of the human dilemma. Here, too, the contrast is total: John accommodates neither simple lack of information (ignorance) nor knowing partly. One knows rightly or not at all.

Nowhere is this emphasis on "knowing" expressed more clearly than in the last sentence of the last summary of Jesus's mission. Here Jesus himself tells God, "Righteous Father, the world does not know (*egno*) you, but I know (*egnon*) you, and these [disciples] know (*egnosan*) that you have sent me. And I made your name known (*egnorisa*) to them, and I will make it known (*gnoriso*)" (17:25–26). This salvific knowing is inseparable from believing, as Simon Peter's confession shows: "We have come to believe and know that you are the Holy One of God" (6:69; see also 16:30 and 17:7–8.).

Not to be taken for granted is what is *not* said: None of what Jesus knows and imparts is called "knowledge" (*gnosis*). John avoids the noun and uses verbs instead.[13] This usage is hardly accidental, for John does not write of "faith" (*pistis*) either, but of believing (*pisteuein*) in God or Jesus. Though this pattern is left unexplained, the Gospel as a whole indicates that this "knowing" is neither a fervent, emotional allegiance with little conceptual content nor a passionless gathering of factual information, but a relational knowing that commits the self in an ongoing relation to God.

God's Exegete

The Gospel's prologue tells readers what to look for in the narrative that follows: the exegesis of the unseen (and unseeable!) God by the only exegete qualified to do so. In accord with Christology's theological correlate, this qualification is rooted in the exegete's relation to God. In John, this relationship is not a matter of Jesus's biography, piety, or religious experience, but of his true identity. Understanding this correlate in John entails considering his preexistence as the Logos, his enfleshment as Jesus, and the sort of exegesis that occurred.

The Exegete's Preexistence

The prologue celebrates the exegete's relation to God because this is the paramount, pervasive, unifying theme of Jesus's message. Whether the prologue was expanded when, or before, it was added to the Gospel (or to an earlier form of it) need not be decided here. It is the present prologue's effect on the Gospel as a whole that matters. Taking the prologue seriously entails reading the selective Jesus stories (20:30–31) as the account of the enfleshed Logos who bivouacked among us, and the results of his doing so. Without the prologue, the account is preposterous; with it, the account is comprehensible—and still astonishing.

The prologue appropriates the Wisdom theology in biblical and hellenistic Jewish thought. Philo had asserted that "Sophia [Wisdom] is the Logos of God" (*Legum Allegoriae* I 65). The Wisdom of Solomon also equated them in saying that God made everything through the Logos, and by Sophia formed humanity (9:1). But whereas Wisdom of Solomon 7:25–26 elaborated Sophia's identity by calling her the breath of God's power, the emanation of God's glory, and the radiation of eternal light, the prologue simply asserts that the Logos "was in the beginning," adding that the Logos was *"with God,"* indeed *"was God."* The prologue neither says nor implies where the Logos came from or came to be with God. Later gnostics will replace this prudent silence with their own explanations.

Important is the prologue's assertion that everything, without exception, owes its existence to the Logos, God's agent in creating. Consequently, when people encounter the Word enfleshed as Jesus they meet their creator as redeemer or as judge. The stakes could hardly be higher or the effects deeper.

Significantly, the prologue does not say *what* the Logos *is*; it speaks instead of *where* he is: "with God." The difference invites comment. A definition provides precise information required for genuine discourse. But both the prologue and the rest of the Gospel imply a restored and renewed relation *to* God requires more than correct information *about* God. Agreeing that "like produces like," the prologue assumes that the preexistent Logos's relation to God grounds the enfleshed Word's ability to convey life to others. A reality less than God cannot do all that God does.

So the prologue ends by restating the colorless "with God" in the vivid language of family relationships: "The only Son, who is in the Father's lap." Only he can exegete the God that no one has ever seen.

At the Last Supper, as noted above, Philip turned the dilemma of the unseen God into a request: "Show us the Father, and we will be satisfied." Indeed! But Jesus rebukes him, "Have I been with you all the time, Philip, [Since 1:43–46!] and you still do not know *me*? Whoever has seen *me* has seen the Father." The prologue makes this remarkable claim intelligible.

Still, it was not the preexistent Logos with God who exegeted God but the Logos enfleshed in Jesus.

The Enfleshment

It is not easy to comprehend the pivotal assertion as a whole: "the Logos became *sarx* [flesh] and bivouacked among us, and we have seen his glory." How one understands the compact statement affects the way one interprets the whole narrative. Rudolph Bultmann emphasized the first part ("the Word became flesh") and so argued that "the revealer is nothing other than a man," and that the revelation is hidden because the incarnation is a paradox. Ernst Käsemann emphasized the second clause ("we have seen his glory") and concluded that in John the humanity of Jesus "recedes into the background" (156). Later, in his Yale Shaffer Lectures, he said John's Christology comes close to a "naive Docetism." Georg Richter (who regarded verses 14–18 as a later addition to the prologue) said Käsemann got verse 14 exactly backward: it was added to *oppose* the naive Docetism of the earlier form of the Gospel; verses 14–18, said Richter, agree with 1 John, which declares that "every spirit that confesses that Jesus Christ has come in the flesh is from God" and views those who deny this as the antichrist (1 John 4:2–3). These views are unsatisfactory because they do not grasp clearly enough the logic of this Gospel.

To understand the *logic* of incarnation (particularly in John), it is necessary to take the word "incarnation" at face value, even though John does not actually use it. It does not mean personification, as in "she was compassion itself." Rather, "became" (*egeneto*) refers to an *event* in which one reality occurs as another. Thus, the term requires assuming that there are two modes of reality, and that mode A existed before becoming mode B. That is, preexistence is required for all incarnation Christology. In John, incarnation as event does not imply that A became B so completely that no trace of A remained; were that the case, A would simply disappear into B, and then the whole point of asserting the Word's enfleshment in the first place would also disappear (as seems to be the case in Bultmann's interpretation). Moreover, in enfleshment logic everything depends on *what* preexisted before becoming enfleshed. In John, the preexistent Logos is more than an idea or intent *in* God, the way a plan exists in the strategist's mind. The Logos was a discrete entity *with* God, sharing God's mode of reality, which contrasts with that of the flesh. Remarkably, the enfleshed Logos retains his preexistent timelessness while in the temporal creation, for in 8:5 he asserts, "Before Abraham was, I *am*." That the enfleshed Logos also remembers his preexistence is no less remarkable.

John does not need to say when or where the Logos was enfleshed; what matters are the consequences of it having occurred. Ironically, the one who made God known must himself be made known by God, as the witness of the baptizer shows (1:19–34). Theologically, Matthew 16:17 makes the same point. Philip, though a disciple from the start (1:43–44), still had not "seen" God because the enfleshment made the Logos a truly human phenomenon, indistinguishable in appearance from others while utterly unique in origin and "nature." Accordingly, the truth is simultaneously concealed and disclosed.[14]

In this Gospel no one denies or doubts that the miraculous "signs" happened. In fact, Nicodemus affirms them as evidence that God is "with" Jesus (3:2). Still, this is inadequate Christology because Jesus's true identity, on which his significance depends, cannot be inferred only from what is observed. It must also be disclosed if one is to understand what *is* observed. The Gospel makes this clear at the outset: God tells the baptizer what the descended visible dove means (1:31–34). Later Jesus himself asserts and expounds his true identity. Readers who accept the prologue's assertions know why Jesus's opponents are regularly wrong about his identity while being right about "the facts."

Is it too much to ask whether the prologue uses mythological language to appropriate metaphysical assumptions for its Christology?

The Enfleshed Exegete

Werner Kelber concluded that "the Logos manifests his identity in difference" because he both "*was* God" and "with God" (in Segovia, 136). Kelber also observed that during the Logos's earthly career the difference is enlarged, while the identity remains unchanged. These insights can be elaborated by asking, What became of the God-relatedness during the enfleshment? It was retained but expressed in two different ways: as the Father's presence with the Son and as the Son's dependence on the Father. Together, they spell out the theological correlate of John's Christology.

During the incarnate state, the preexistent Logos's presence "with God" is reversed; now God is *with Jesus.* Thus, Jesus asserts, "And he who sent me is with me; he has not left me alone, for I always do what is pleasing to him" (8:29). At the Supper, Jesus foresees abandonment and says, "Yet I am not alone, for the Father is with me" (16:32). That God is "with" someone means that the person acts as God's valid agent, as was said of Moses (Exodus 3:12), Jeremiah (Jeremiah 1:19), and Jesus (John 3:2). But in the mouth of the enfleshed Logos, God's "withness" implies unbroken solidarity between the heavenly Father and his earthly Son.

The Gospel translates the prologue's distinction between God *ho theos* and Logos *theos* into their paralleled actions. So Jesus can say, "Whatever the Father does, the Son does likewise. Indeed, just as the Father raises the dead and gives them life, so also the Son gives life to whomever he wishes" (5:19, 21). This parallelism warrants Jesus's capacity to exegete God; that is, because Jesus does what God does, to see Jesus rightly is to see God as well. Jesus's reply to Philip is central in this Gospel's Christology.

Moreover, given the "otherness" of flesh, it is not surprising that the enfleshment is envisioned as *descent* into unfriendly environment. In 6:38 Jesus himself says, "I have come down from heaven."

By being enfleshed the Logos also became *dependent* on God. This dependence is expressed in several ways. First, Jesus claims he was sent by God. "I came from God and now I am here. I did not come on my own, but he sent me" (8:42). Thus, he came in his *Father's* name (5:43), not in his own.[15]

Second, Jesus asserts that he says what he heard from God (8:26, 40). At the Supper he tells the disciples, "I have made known to you everything that I heard from the Father" (15:15). In his prayer he tells God, "The words that you gave to me I have given to them" (17:8). He has no independent message.

Finally, Jesus expresses his dependence also when he talks of glorifying the Father by finishing the work God gave him to do (17:4). Likewise, he honors the Father (8:49) and does what pleases him (8:29). He insists he does not seek his own glory (8:50), for "if I glorify myself, my glory is nothing" (verse 54). Indeed, the mission of Jesus is viewed as the reciprocal glorification of the Father and the Son, climaxed in Jesus's death.

God Exegeted

The discussion now turns from the *theo*logical to the anthropological/ soteriological correlate in John. Now the overarching question is *What did the enfleshed Logos achieve for humankind's benefit?* Without an appropriate and adequate answer, what John says about Christ's identity is merely interesting. With it, John's Christology can become religiously relevant.

John's answer is as bold as it is challenging: the gift of (true) life to the living (and dead) through the enfleshed Word's exegesis of God. Comprehending this answer entails considering the exegesis of God, as such, the life given, and the exegesis of God after the enfleshment has ended.

On Exegeting God

The exegesis of God is mentioned only at the end of the prologue. As the last Greek word in the prologue's last sentence, *exegēsato* states the positive import of the Christ event. But what is meant by what is said here?

The prologue is not its own exegete. Nor does it explain. It celebrates. In doing so it omits what is not needed and highlights what is pivotal. It also puts its many assertions into a deliberate sequence. By announcing the enfleshment well before reporting the Son's exegeting action, the prologue implies that the incarnation itself is not the saving event but the necessary antecedent to it. Similarly, mentioning the Son's exegeting after asserting the failure to see God implies that this exegesis resolves Philip's plight of not seeing God. Thus, in juxtaposing these two statements the prologue instantiates the anthropological/soteriological correlate in John's Christology.

The failure to see God is persistent, universal, and ubiquitous, not transitory, culture-specific (a Jewish or Roman failure), or regional. It is not a tolerable prelude to successes either. It is a *condition* infecting and affecting human life as a whole. Here no appeal to good intent ("they meant well") or good effort ("they tried hard") ameliorates this state of affairs.

When Jesus occasionally comments on the human condition, he uses metaphors of danger and destruction. Thus, in declaring, "Everyone who commits sin is slave to sin," he interprets the condition as unintended consequence of transgression: bondage. Here no contingency ameliorates the seriousness of this outcome. The declaration does not differentiate an egregious transgression from a misdemeanor or recognize a difference between a single misdeed and a habitual one. Nor does the assertion show concern for others, those affected by the sin; its focus is not on the deed but on the doer who has lost the ability not to sin.

A comparable assessment is expressed when Jesus speaks of "this world" (*kosmos*). Saying "this world" does not specify which world is in view; it expresses a negative, derogatory value judgment. Further, since *kosmos* ordinarily refers to the entire empirical universe, when used metaphorically for the human condition it implies that the condition as a universal debilitating environment. Within it one lives as a subservient subject from which one cannot emigrate at will. Thus, Jesus pictures it as a domain with an illegitimate sovereign: "Now is the judgment of this world. Now shall the ruler of this world be cast out" (12:31). At the Supper he says that "the ruler of this world is coming. He has no power over me" (14:30).

In an allusion to Adam and Eve in Eden, Jesus calls the devil a murderer from the start as well as a liar and the "father (begetter) of lies" (8:44), but he does not really explain the nature and origin of the human predicament. Explanation was not his vocation. Had it been, the Son's exegesis of God would have been quite different.

The prologue implies that one must distinguish exegeting God from exegeting God talk (and talking about God talk!) Only exegeting the God reality itself heals the human *condition*. Exegeting God talk can clarify, challenge, and correct concepts of God (a good result), but it cannot do what exegeting *God* does: mend the broken, severed, distorted relation *to* God.

The prologue assumes that the referent of the word "God" is not the super-being in a hierarchy of beings but their ground, indeed the "ground of being" as such. Exegeting this entity differs, therefore, from exegeting any other entity. It also requires an equally unique exegete, as noted. Here, what is definitive is the obvious: this exegesis of God occurs through an event, a human life—concretely, through the enfleshed Word's self-proclamation and self-giving. The enfleshed Son exegetes the ground of being by the way he lives among beings caught in the human condition. Thus, the *life* in the preexistent Logos becomes *life-giving* in the "work" of the existent Jesus.

Exactly how this becomes transformative in believers is left unsaid, and so is unmanipulable. But the transformation—its character and consequences—can be glimpsed in what this Gospel says about the engendered life.

The Life Engendered

John does not provide a neutral observer's description or an analysis of the life generated by the enfleshed Logos. Instead, it uses common metaphors for its uncommon traits and vivid images for the changes its inauguration effects. Nor does the Gospel portray or imply the life of any specific disciple; the beloved disciple is not the model. Rather, this portrait discloses what is logically true, not what is empirically accurate, as a glance at the Johannine Epistles will confirm. What is said about the new life is its norm, functioning as promise and obligation, not as a portrait of achievements.

Moreover, given John's either/or thinking on the one hand, and its habit of ignoring extenuating circumstances on the other, it is not surprising that the life portrayed lacks what is central in most realistic novels: ambiguity and ambivalence. Nor does John regard this eternal life as a quest or pilgrimage. It is a gift received already.

The imparted life remains undefined, but its character can be discerned in the various metaphors used to interpret and commend it. Diverse as they are, they all assume that this life differs fundamentally from ordinary life. The difference is constitutive, not comparative. It is not simply "another" life; it is life that is radically "other." It is "eternal," not merely everlasting. Whatever is eternal is "other" and so cannot be truly defined with categories and concepts crafted for understanding phenomena in time. What these sentences say abstractly is conveyed vividly by John in what happened at the tomb of Lazarus (chapter 11).

In this complex story Jesus first uses belief in future resurrection to comfort Martha. But when she agrees he confronts her with an astounding claim: "I am the resurrection and the life." *This* resurrection is here, available now by believing Jesus's words about himself. Her response is a paradigmatic Christological confession: "You are the Christ, the Son of God who comes [present tense] into the world." Then, upon arriving at the tomb, he summons Lazarus back to life as a "sign" (not a demonstration) of transformative resurrection. Lazarus is restored to status quo ante, Martha receives life that is "other."

The "otherness" of this life ruptures the ordinary meaning of ordinary words and relies on their metaphorical meanings. For instance, it spawned the riddle Jesus gave to Martha as a follow-up to his self-proclamation: "Those who believe in me, though they die, will live, and everyone who lives and believes in me will never die. Do you believe this?"

In chapter 6 Jesus uses metaphors that jar the imagination in order to illuminate the nexus of Christ, life, and believing. Jesus not only speaks of "the bread of God . . . which comes down from heaven and gives life to the world" (6:34); he also declares, "I am the bread of life."

"The Jews" find this claim preposterous, for they know his parents but not John's prologue. But Jesus presses on. "I am the living bread that comes down from heaven. Whoever eats this bread will live forever; and the bread that I will give for the life of the world is my flesh" (6:51)—a deliberate paradox because flesh cannot convey immortality. Again, a dispute.

But now Jesus launches into the most remarkable self-proclamation in the whole Gospel: "I tell you, unless you eat the flesh of the Son of Man, and drink his blood, you have no life in you. Those who eat my flesh and drink my blood have eternal life, and I will raise them up on the last day" (6:53–54). Thus, everything that Jesus had said about himself metaphorically as the bread of life is now enacted by literally eating the eucharist (the participle *trogon* means chew, munch).

Remarkably, this Gospel does not report the Lord's Supper but only the Last Supper. Was it omitted because the whole Gospel is sacramental? Or is this Gospel antisacramental? Both miss the point. John has no story of Jesus instituting the eucharist because the eucharist is grounded not in a discrete deed on a given night but in the whole event of Jesus as the enfleshed Logos. The flow of blood and water from the pierced side of the Crucified makes the same point: eucharist and baptism are grounded in Jesus himself, at the apex of his mission, where the enfleshment is most palpable. Jesus's word about chewing his flesh implies that the reality and meaning of the incarnation must be internalized, digested. Otherwise, there is no life *in* us.

Instead of explaining the believer's life, the prologue accounts for its "otherness" by speaking metaphorically of its origin. To all who received the enfleshed Logos and believed in his name "he gave *exousia* [legitimate authority/power] to become children of God." Another metaphor says how this transforming transition comes about: by being "born of God"[16]—a kind of birth that differs completely from one traced to human will. Also, whatever is born *of* God is derived *from* God and is determined *by* God. In other words, what God as "Ground of being" means is actualized in human contingency. Given the brokenness of humanity's relation to God, restoring *this* contingency is redemptive.

Jesus's role in the engendered life is often expressed metaphorically in the "I am" sayings that have a predicate. (The simple "I am," *egō eimi*, appropriates God's self-identification to Moses.)

bread	6:35
light	8:12
gate	10:7
shepherd	10:11
resurrection	11:25
way	14:16
vine	15:1

Though not clustered into a programmatic unit like the Beatitudes in Matthew, taken together they outline the relationship between the Life-giver and the life given, between the enfleshed Word's life and the engendered life in the believer. None of these sayings states an ideal goal to be pursued; all of them announce what is true inherently, not incidentally or incrementally true. The declaration's beneficial meaning is spelled out concisely in the comment that follows the saying, as in 8:12: "I am the light of [for] the world. Those who follow me will never walk in darkness but will have the light of [for] life," that is, eternal life.

Jesus does not say that he is light or *a* light. He claims to be *the* light of the world. He recognizes no competitor. Significantly, the explanatory comments also come from Jesus himself: they are neither the narrator's nor a disciple's interpretation. They are Jesus's own exposition of his metaphorical interpretation of his role in the believer's engendered life. In short, he is his own exegete. In fact, he explains why he speaks in metaphors (16:25), and why he did not tell his followers everything: They "cannot bear them now" (16:12), that is, before his mission is completed. Implicit in the present tense of the saying is the promise that what is true now will be true in the future also. In prefacing some sayings with "truly, truly, I say," he guarantees it.

In this Gospel especially, the believer's life is *Christomorphic* because it is deliberately *Christocentric*. To believe Jesus or believe in him is to be shaped by him. Everything therefore depends on the character of the shaper. In John, only the Word enfleshed as Jesus can impart and nourish the kind of life Martha received when she believed Jesus's claim "I am the resurrection and the life." *This* life is not to be identified with "Christian ethics." Its focus is the doer rather than the deed and its effects, as already noted.

The "I am" sayings' implicit exclusiveness manifests the Christocentric feature of the believer's life; its Christomorphic character is centered in "following" Jesus. Fundamental is what Jesus says at the Supper: "I have given you an example, that you also should do as I have done to you by washing your feet" (13:15). This simple self-humbling act epitomizes Jesus's whole life as one of self-giving to and for others.

The story of the foot washing lets us see as well as understand what following Jesus means *in John*. The setting of the reported action is described precisely, but the act itself is not described at all. Though Passover implicitly anchors the event in chronological time, its kairological time is stated explicitly: Jesus's imminent departure from the world, in which the disciples will remain. What Jesus says to the twelve in the narrative is also addressed to all followers in the world after his work is completed.

The story emphasizes what Jesus did before and after washing the disciples' feet: after the (undescribed) meal, he "rose from the supper," exchanged his robe for a towel, and began the washing. Upon completing the action, he reversed his preparatory acts, returning to the place he had left. In this story, then, the whole foot washing event acts out the U-shape of the Christ event's preexistence, existence, postexistence. In this drama the foot washing act is the nadir of the Word's self-abasement. Further, the moral meaning of this Christological drama is enacted in the disciples' service to each other.

Apparently, following Jesus does not include bearing one's own cross. This Gospel has no equivalent of Matthew 16:24: "If anyone wants to become my follower, let them deny themselves and take up their cross and follow me." John's Jesus does, to be sure, foresee suffering and martyrdom for his future disciples (9:22, 12:42, 16:1–2), but he does not require them to seek either one. Put tersely, the disciples' life is to be Christomorphic, but not cruciform.

Jesus's death is voluntary: "No one takes it from me, but I lay it down of my own accord. I have *exousia* (the right) to lay it down and I have the *exousia* to take it up again. I have received this command from my Father" (10:18). Jesus will die neither as a martyr for a cause nor as a victim, but as the obedient Son carrying out the Father's will freely, not as a fate.

In John, the whole earthly sojourn of the enfleshed Logos is the saving event, whose purpose is completed in Jesus's death, as his triumphal final word announces, "It is completed!" Jesus's task is done, and now he returns to the Father who sent him, leaving his followers "in" but not "of" the world, as he had been. At the Supper he foretold what they can expect.

Exegesis Post Jesum

In the Farewell Discourses (as chapters 13–14 are labeled), Jesus emphasizes the positive results of his departure: "It is to your advantage that I go away" (16:7). Thus, he discourages those who had accompanied him from wallowing in self-pity and dissuades future followers from wishing they could have seen and heard what the first followers had experienced. It is better to be a believer by responding to the preached story of Jesus's work than to have seen and heard it all without comprehending what was seen and heard. After Easter Jesus reinforces the point: "Blessed are those who have not seen and yet have come to believe" (20:29).

Jesus speaks of three significant advantages. For one thing, the believer enjoys a new relation to God that is possible only when Jesus's work is completed: "Those who love me will keep my word, and my Father will love them, and we will come to them and make our home with them" (14:23); the enfleshment's temporary bivouacking is to be replaced by the residing of both the Father and the Son. That, Jesus implies, can happen only after the enfleshment has ended.

In addition, "the one who believes in me will also do the works that I do, and, in fact, will do greater works than these, because I am going to the Father" (14:12). What these greater works are is not specified (fortunately). Implicitly, then, the faith elicited by the preached, interpreting word is greater than that eliciting by the ambiguous signs themselves.

The third advantage may be the most significant. The transient, temporal enfleshment of the timeless Logos will be followed by the arrival of a successor, the Paraclete, the Holy Spirit, who "will be with you forever" (14:16). The Paraclete can come only if Jesus departs, as Jesus himself insists (16:7). The Paraclete is "the Spirit of truth, whom the world cannot receive because it neither sees him nor knows him. You know him, because he abides with you and will be in [or, among] you" (14:16–17). And the Spirit (a) "will teach you everything, and (b) remind you of all that I have said to you." The two functions must be seen together. Indeed, each prevents the misuse of the other. By itself the first can easily become a slogan of a movement that claims its teachings go beyond what Jesus had taught. The second can easily warrant an anxious traditionalism. (The Johannine Epistles imply that both tendencies were a problem, as noted.) Taken together, these promises assure the community that the Spirit/Paraclete will replace but never displace Jesus.

An accurate translation of *paraklētos* (used for the Spirit only in John) remains elusive. Words ordinarily used—advocate, counselor, helper—do not match precisely what the Paraclete is said to do. It is the activity of the Spirit that tells readers who the Paraclete is, not the lexicon's definition of the word. In other words, in pneumatology as in Christology, meaning is expressed in sentences, not in isolated nouns.

Jesus forgoes a comprehensive overview of the Paraclete's work and accents what is essential. Nothing is said about ecstasy as evidence of the Spirit's arrival; John shows no interest in the Spirit as power, as in the Book of Acts, or in the Spirit as "down payment" for full salvation as does Paul. For John, the Spirit as permanent gift is a didactic, not a charismatic presence.

According to John, the faith community that lives by the Spirit will never outgrow Jesus, for the Spirit does not take us beyond him but only ever more deeply into the event in which the Logos became flesh among us.

⚜ 6 ⚜

HEBREWS

Jesus and the Pilgrim's Assurance

Nothing is so calculated to enslave the mind as fear of death through a desire to live.

—Philo

The main characteristic of most "utopias" is the fact that they are static. Nothing is then altered, for they have reached perfection.

—Isaiah Berlin

HEBREWS, THE MOST polished literary product of the most urbane mind in the New Testament, fascinates some readers and bores others—and for the same reason: This document's ideas, and its ways of expressing them, seem wholly alien to our own religious concerns. It may, however, have the most challenging—and therefore rewarding—Christology in the New Testament.

Its content *is* peculiar. Though interested in the rituals of sacrifice, it ignores the Jerusalem temple completely and concentrates on ancient Israel's tent sanctuary that no one had seen for centuries. Hebrews also relies on an obscure figure in Genesis 14 to interpret Christ. Besides, it is the only book in the New Testament that develops a Christology centered in Christ's priesthood, yet points out that Jesus was not a priest, for he was of the wrong tribe. Also, no other New Testament writing is as interested in Christ's *post*existence in heaven, nor does any other New Testament book emphasize more the saving significance of Jesus's humanness. In the New Testament, only Romans matches its capacity to combine relentless argument and pastoral concern. Indeed, the more one notes and ponders its uniqueness, the more intriguing its Christology becomes.

The So-Called Letter to the So-Called Hebrews

The Homilist and His Hearers

Those who first heard the homily—a hortatory address—read aloud may have been surprised that it ended as a letter. It certainly did not begin like a letter, naming the sender and identifying the recipient. Hebrews does neither. Its creator never identifies himself by name nor by status (e.g., apostle, elder); instead, he totally recedes in the text, defeating scholars' efforts to identify who he was. They do, however, know what he was: a sophisticated, educated Christian theologian well read in the Greek Bible, self-assured enough to assume that he need not state his qualifications or write in someone else's name. Here it is the word spoken that commends the speaker.[1]

Despite the oversupply of scholars' hypotheses, the first readers' identity remains as unknown as the author's. The greeting from "those from Italy" (13:24) no more discloses where either the greeters or the greeted live than the title "to Hebrews," added early, gives us their ethnic identity. However, the title, inferred from the content, has been used to support the inference that Hebrews was addressed to Christian Jews who were in danger of returning to Judaism. There is no evidence for this view either. Assuming that return to ancestral religion would have been attractive before the temple was destroyed, some also inferred that Hebrews was written before that catastrophe occured. But "scholars are equally divided between those who think an origin before . . . 70 CE 'impossible' and those who think an origin after 70 CE 'inconceivable.'"[2] Käsemann's tart comment should not have been ignored: Getting rid of the notion of relapse to Judaism "would be like being liberated from a malevolent ghost."[3] For the record, this chapter assumes that Hebrews was written after 80 CE but before 95, when it appears to be referred to in 1 Clement, written then in Rome (some therefore infer that Hebrews was originally sent to Roman believers).

The homily's admonitions provide promising clues to how the author viewed its recipients, and what he wanted it to achieve. The homilist did not remind his readers of the nature or history of his relation to them (as did Paul in 1 Corinthians 2:1–5 and 1 Thessalonians 1:2–12, for example), nor did he say how he learned their current situation. Nor does their pre-Christian past play any role in the discussion. He simply refers to their conversion as receiving "the knowledge of the truth" (10:26) and as having been "once enlightened" (6:4; 10:32), presumably by the message confirmed by those who heard the Lord's word "from the beginning, which God also attested by marvels and the Holy Spirt" (2:3–4, my translation).[4]

More important is the distinction seen between their previous *Christian* life and their current state. The homilist asks the readers to recall "the former days" when they endured much difficulty, specified as a public humiliation, affliction, solidarity with prisoners, and seizure of property (10:32–34), though no loss of blood (12:4). When these experiences occurred or what prompted them is not said. What matters is the difference between "then" and "now" (though not totally different, see 6:10).

In 5:11–14 the author faults them for arrested development: by now they should be teachers instead of still needing to be taught; they should be eating solid food instead of needing milk. Not only do they need to be taught again the basics of God's word, but the homilist attributes his difficulty in explain his thought to *their* having become obtuse ("dull in understanding"). Their immaturity, he implies, has also weakened their moral competence; now it needs training in making moral judgments (literally, to distinguish good and evil).

Because the homilist views Christian existence as a journey (see below), many admonitions urge continuing effort: holding fast (3:6, 14; 4:14; 10:23), striving (4:11, 12:14), running (12:1), overcoming

exhaustion (12:12). Other comments point out the unintended consequences of not striving: drifting away (2:1), neglect (2:2), falling (4:10),
becoming sluggish (6:12), getting fatigued and faint-hearted (12:3) or
bitter (12:14), as well as staying away from worship (10:25) and being
enticed by strange teachings (13:9). Still others counsel against turning away from God (*apostenai* can also imply apostasy from doctrine),
sinning deliberately (12:26), refusing to heed God's word (12:25), and
throwing away faith's boldness (10:35).

Stated bluntly, "you need endurance" so that, having done God's
will, you will duly receive the promised salvation (10:36). In short,
the homilist urges, "Lift up the drooping hands and strengthen your
week knees, and make straight the paths for your feet, so that what is
lame may not be put out of joint [i.e., your condition not get worse],
but rather be healed" (12:12). Though fearing that the readers may
"drift away" from the faith, the author no more indicates what they
may drift into than he identifies the strange teachings that might lure
them away (13:9). Whatever the (unspecified) attracting alternative,
"drifting away" is itself a great danger because one cannot come back
(6:4–8; 10:26–31).[5]

The author does not help his first readers understand *how* they
came to be in their current state, for he does not explain what "caused"
it. In fact, it is not causes or contributing factors that concern him, but
consequences. Accordingly, he does not blame any person or group
within or outside the community—not even Satan, as do Matthew
13:27–28; Mark 4:15; and 1 Peter 5:8–9. Nor does he scold the readers or hold the congregation's leadership responsible for the community's religious apathy; to the contrary, he urges the readers both to obey
them because "they are keeping watch over your souls" (13:17, RSV)
and to "imitate their faith" (13:8).

Presumably, the readers were "drifting away" because they had
become disappointed with the Christian faith they had avowed and
suffered for. What had grasped them no longer held their attention, as the decline in church attendance implies. Rejuvenating their

faithfulness would require more than urging allegiance to basic ideas, even if the reader needed a remedial course (6:12). After all, avowing those rudiments had not prevented the current plight: drifting away. Needed now was a loyalty that would be "drift proof" because it is warranted by the truth about Christ that is as permanent as Christ himself: "the same yesterday and today and forever" (13:8, alluding to 1:12 [quoting Psalm 102:27]). Indeed, the homilist has a special word to express this enduring import of the Christ event: *ephapax*, once for all time (not merely *hapax*, occurring once); see 7:27; 9:12; and 10:10.

The emphasis on this particular truth about Christ implies that that readers were "drifting away" because they were having their doubts. A careful reading of 2:5–9 suggests why this was happening.

Hebrews 2:5–9 uses Psalm 8:4–6 to interpret Psalm 110:1,[6] which quotes God, "Sit at my right hand until I make your enemies a footstool under your feet." Having implied that God was not saying this to an angel (1:18), the homilist now explains that the subjection described in Psalm 110:1 was spoken to the figure portrayed in Psalm 8, the "son of man," now understood as the preexistent Son who was enthroned at God's right hand after he had been momentarily a human being.[7]

Further, inferring that the "enemies" made into the Son's footstool in Psalm 110:1 (quoted in Hebrews 1:13) refers to the "all things" put under the Son of Man's feet (as Psalm 8 is read in Hebrews 2:8), the homilist now insists that "all things" means exactly what it says: "Now in subjecting all things to him, nothing was left unsubjected" (2:9, my translation). This insistence probably points to the readers' problem: "yet at present we do not see everything set subjected to him"—period.[8] The starkness of this observation must not be softened, for it illumines the readers' disappointment which probably lay behind the "drifting away" that the homily was to arrest and reverse.

What is said next is truly remarkable: Although we do not *see* Christ's universal sovereignty, "we do see Jesus"—precisely the one sketched in Psalm 8, whom God made lower than angels (i.e., a human), for a little while but who is now "crowned with honor and glory" that we do not see.

Lest the "not seeing" call into question the reality of Christ's sovereignty (as may well have been happening), and the "seeing" of Jesus be taken as a mere consolation, a weak substitute, the homilist does something even more remarkable: on the one hand, he will claim that the seen Jesus is both pivotal for the salvific impact of the Christ event and also a model for Christian life; on the other hand, he will tacitly link the "not seen" to the nature of Christian existence in history as journey, not arrival. To do so, he relied on a particular worldview.

The Homily's Conceptual World

Since the homilist neither describes nor defends his worldview, he evidently assumes that his readers shared it. Instructive as it would be to depict its contours and to trace the histories of its diverse elements, a concise summary that illumines what Hebrews says about Christ and the Christian life must suffice here.

For the homilist and his readers there are two kinds of reality. One is the world of everyday experience; it is visible, phenomenal, empirical, tangible, temporal (hence temporary). The other is invisible, ideal, intangible, timeless—a drastically different realm. Earthly phenomena are inferior copies of the "really real" in heaven (or beyond "the heavens"). This view was given its most influential expression by Plato and was also affirmed by the apostle, "What can be seen is temporary, but what cannot be seen is eternal" (1 Corinthians 1:18).

This view of reality was foundational also for the Alexandrian Jewish theological exegete, Philo, a contemporary of Jesus and Paul.[9] In treating the Pentateuch allegorically, he argued that the early chapters of Genesis disclose reality, metaphorical reality. The subsequent stories in Genesis portrayed the soul's journey to blessedness, and the Pentateuch's laws which, when obeyed, discipline the soul on its way. For this discussion, it matters little whether, or to what degree,

Philo influenced the homilist directly. They can sound alike because both were influenced by middle Platonism yet have different agendas. As Charles Carlston noted decades ago, while they lived in the same generally "Platonic" world, "they were citizens of quite different countries."[10] Philo often spelled out what the homilist alludes to while making different claims. For instance, both assumed that the metaphysical, ontic dualism of reality is structural ("the way things are" because God made them that way) and permanent.

The homilist's conceptual world is deeply influenced by another factor as well, one found in Jewish and early Christian apocalyptic thought, viz the two ages (or eons), this age and the Age to come. Whereas the Platonic-Philonic view of reality was "vertical" (heavenly and earthly), sequential two-age thought was "horizontal" (this world and the world to come), though in some apocalyptic thought the coming world already exists in heaven.[11]

Though scholars recognize the presence of these two worldviews in Hebrews, they have not agreed on how they are related—that is, whether the homily makes one more important than the other.[12] In Hebrews, the vertical or cosmological structural worldviews and the horizontal or sequential eschatological view do not simply coexist but affect one another. The vertical, Platonic-Philonic tradition allows the homilist to argue that true salvation is not a phenomenon on earth but an eternal existence in heaven, where God is. The horizontal, sequential dualism of Jewish and early Christian eschatology enables him to claim that the real is coming: "here we have no lasting city, but we are looking for the city to come" (13:14), as well as to view the ancient rites of atonement as more than copies of the real as also anticipations, or foreshadowings. Above all, the interaction of these worldviews enables the homilist to tell the disappointed readers that their salvation is real *because* it is in heaven, not on earth, where it would be a transient good. Ironically, we will see that it is this view of reality that makes the visible Jesus particularly significant in the homily's Christology.

The Homilist's Procedure

The creator of Hebrews responded to the readers' situation by producing a work that he called a "word of exhortation" (13:22), which scholars identify as a "homily," a discourse that is rhetorically designed to persuade and encourage. Though relying on the conventions of ancient rhetoric, Hebrews does not conform completely to the kind of discourses it resembled most—deliberative.[13] Moreover, its repeated oscillation between exposition and exhortation keeps its purpose before both the first readers and today's: to provide the convincing Christological warrant (the *logos* or rationale[14]) for a Christian life that is steadfast because it is securely grounded in invisible, heavenly reality. Moreover, persuading the readers that *this* particular Christology has such warranting capacity requires the homilist to reason *toward* it, and to use commonly accepted ways of arguing.[15] Further, persuasion is more feasible when the speaker and the hearer acknowledge the same authority to which one can appeal without legitimating it first. For the homilist that authority is twofold: Scripture and uncontested elements in the Christian tradition.

In creating this homily for fellow believers, the homilist appeals only to the Greek Bible. He quotes no Christian figure or writing. Even when he quotes God's Son, he uses the words of Scripture, not the words of Jesus in a gospel or oral tradition (2:12–13). Christian writings might not yet have come to be widely regarded as "Scripture." Besides, since the Greek Bible contains what God said, the homilist believes that God still speaks in those words (e.g., 1:6, 8:7). Consequently, the homily shows little interest in what the Bible meant in the past.

Hebrews does not correlate Scripture's word with incidents in Jesus's life or teaching. The fulfillment that matters is the new covenant promised in Jeremiah 31. Nor does Hebrews show any interest in *Heilsgeschichte* (salvation history), for it virtually ignores Israel's history. The roster of exemplary Old Testament figures in chapter 11 does, of course, present them in chronological sequence, but the sequence itself does not constitute either a *history* of salvation or a *salvation* history.

What this chapter reports are repeated, often unconnected, instantiations of faithfulness in times of duress. Indeed, "all of these died in faith *without* having received the promises" (11:13)—an *Unheilsgeschichte*. That is the reason the account was assembled in the first place. Although references to Christian martyrs (Stephen, Jesus's brother James, Peter, Paul) could have extended the roster of heroes, the homilist shows no interest in their fidelity either. Remarkably, the homilist never mentions or alludes to any specific thing Jesus did (6:6, 12:2).

In light of these observations, it is instructive to note what Hebrews does say about Jesus. He knows that "our Lord descended from [the tribe of] Judah" (7:13), a datum that is important because it shows that Jesus was not a priest by descent in the tribe of Levi. The homilist also knows that Jesus preached the message of salvation (2:3), but its content is not stated; when he does quote Jesus, the words are addressed to God, and quote two Old Testament passages (2:12–13, citing Psalm 22:22 and Isaiah 8:17), as referring to Christ's mission (10:5–7, citing Psalm 40:6–8). He knows that Jesus was tempted (4:14, 2:18) in every way (4:14, 2:18) but does not need to say when this occurred, or what tempted him. The two references to the cross (6:6, 12:2) do not speak of it as a saving event as does Paul (e.g., 1 Corinthian 1:18, 2:2). Not until 13:20 does the homily say that God "brought" Jesus from the dead; the customary words for his resurrection appear only in 6:2 (part of the elementary teaching that does not mention Jesus) and 11:25 (which refer to martyrs restored to life). As in Philippians 2:9, Jesus's death is followed by his exaltation; unlike Luke-Acts, his resurrection is not followed by his ascension. Hebrews expects Christ's "second" coming, this time to save those who expect him (9:28); this will occur soon (10:27), as will the judgment (the "day" in 9:25).

It is futile to guess what else the homilist knew about Jesus. Fruitful instead is noting how much the homilist can say about the soteriological significance of precisely "the Jesus of history" (not "the historical Jesus") without narrating any incident in his life or quoting what Jesus said about his death, though that death is essential for his Christology.

This Christology can simply affirm Christ's identity as "Son," but it must explain his role as priest in order to show Christ's relevance. That is, "priest" points to this Christology's anthropological/soteriological correlate, while "Son" summarizes its theological correlate. Even so, "priest" is not used as a Christological title. Hebrews never calls Jesus "the priest."

In producing Hebrews, the homilist became the only New Testament theologian to state the rationale that makes any Christology plausible—viz, the solidarity of the Savior and the saved. Without this, three-phase Christology will not "work." Hebrews (2:10–18) states the essential point succinctly: since humans are *made* of flesh and blood, "he himself shared the same things"; indeed, "he had to be made like them, fully human in every way" (NIV) in order to become "a merciful and faithful high priest in the service of God, to make a sacrifice of atonement for the sins of the people" (2:14, 17 NRSV). Whereas some forms of Christian gnosticism held that the Savior and the saved always shared the same nature (preexistence), in Hebrews the solidarity is achieved by an event, the incarnation.

Classical Christology has often emphasized Christ's significance through the "offices" of prophet, priest, and king. Whereas "prophet" accents Christ's role as definitive articulator of God's will and way, and "king" emphasizes his sovereign rule, "priest" focuses the redeemer's role in removing the sin that prevents access to the holy God. In Hebrews, sin produces defilement, requiring purification (as 1:3 implies) not propitiation. Using cultic sacrificial categories to interpret Christ inevitably produces a Christology that concentrates on one's access to God.[16]

The Anthropological/Soteriological Correlate

Comprehending this correlation entails considering three of its components: the human condition affected by Christ's priestly act, the new "economy of salvation," and the believers' journey to God.

The Human Condition Overcome

In Hebrews the human condition is never described, explained, or accounted for by locating its origins. Adam and Eve are not mentioned. For the homily, it is the consequences, not the causes, that must be addressed. Diverse aspects of the human condition can, however, be inferred from what is said about the salvation effected by Christ. Sometimes the homily weaves discrete motifs into a concise statement of the human condition and its resolution in Christ. Hebrews 2:14–15 is such a passage, tantalizing partly because it leaves much unsaid and partly because it remains undeveloped in the rest of the homily.

In this passage, the Son's enfleshment occurred "so that through the death [viz, his; NRSV omits 'the'] he might destroy the one who has the power of death, that is, the devil, and free those who all their lives were held in slavery by the fear of death." Here the enslavement is not to the fact of death (human mortality), as in Romans, but to a hostile alien power (the devil, mentioned only here) who uses one's internal, emotional response to the fact of one's death to maintain control. Since the fear of death is lifelong, it manifests an aspect or the human condition.[17]

Hebrews does not explain what prompted the fear of death, but 9:27 may provide a clue: humans are destined to face God's judgment (see also12:23) after dying—a dreadful prospect if one has not been purified from sin. Moreover, God's swordlike word penetrates to the self's innermost recesses, enabling God to "judge the thoughts and intentions of the heart," not only one's actual transgressions. Human vulnerability in God's court is universal: "All are naked . . . to the eyes of the one to whom he must render an account" (4:12–13).

This interest in fear shows the homily's concern for the "psychological" aspect of the human condition, that is, how it affects one's self-awareness (and self-image). Accordingly, this concern will influence the homily's understanding of how Christ's death dealt with sin's defiling impact.

The discussion of the Son's priesthood and self-sacrifice is rather well developed, indicating that the homily regards defilement as the more important aspect of the human condition. Indeed, "purification for sins" is the first thing said about the Son's soteriological significance (1:3).

The homily has various ways of expressing this theme, for example, "bearing" the sins of others (9:28), "removing" their sin (9:26; 10:4, 11), making "a sacrifice of atonement for the sins of the people" (2:17), "cleansing" 10:22). However formulated, this saving action occurred "by the sacrifice of himself" (10:26). All such language assumes that "without the shedding of blood there is no forgiveness of sin" (9:22).

In such language, moreover, sin is imaged as an entity, something that can be dealt with "objectively"; it can be "carried" and "removed" as a burden. Though never defined, explained, or accounted for, sin is a reality that mars the self and prevents access to God until it is dealt with adequately. And that requires a redeeming action that can deal with the defilement of the whole person, that can "cleanse the heart of its evil conscience" (10:21; also 9:14). Without actually saying so, Hebrews views the human condition so negatively because the homilist is concerned that the sacrificial system prescribed in Scripture cannot do what is required.

With especially the Day of Atonement rituals (prescribed in Leviticus 16) in view, the homilist identifies five aspects of the Old Testament sacrificial system that render it religiously insufficient and finally incompetent. *First*, the whole action takes place not in the realm of the really real but in "a sanctuary made by human hands, a mere copy of the true one." In making his sacrifice, Christ "entered heaven itself" (9:24, 8:5). *Second*, the annual repetition of the ritual shows that its benefits are only temporary, those sacrifices are actually a reminder of sin year after year (10:3). But Christ's action occurred *ephapax* (9:26), thereby achieving it as an "eternal redemption" (9:12). *Third*, whereas the high priest enters the holiest inner sanctum of the wilderness tent "with blood that is not his own" (9:24), Christ entered God's presence "not with the blood of goats and calves, but with his own blood" (9:14). *Fourth*, the high priest's sacrifices "cannot perfect the conscience of the worshiper, but deal only with . . . regulations for the body imposed until the time comes to set things right" (9:9–10)—that is, until the new economy of salvation arrives in Christ. *Fifth*, it is inherently "impossible for the blood of bulls and goats to take away sin" (10:4). In fact, when the Son "came into the world," he himself told God, "Sacrifices and offering you have not desired" (using words from Psalm 40:6–8). What did please God, the homilist implies, was the Son's doing God's will, freely.[18] And the Son's obedience brought about both an unflawed redemption and nothing less than a new economy of salvation.

The New Economy of Salvation

Together the priest, his actions and the character of the purification constitute a coherent whole. Therefore, the homilist can argue that "when there is a change in the priesthood [not a mere change in staff], there is necessarily a change in the law [the legitimating system] as well" (7:13). Not only was Christ's priesthood such a change, but it was also foreshadowed in Scripture, where it appeared as *Melchizedek*.[19]

In Genesis 14 Melchizedek appears suddenly as the priest who blessed Abraham, victorious in recent battles. Abraham in turn gave him a tenth of the spoils. For the homilist, this obscure incident is theologically significant because of what God said in Psalm 110. Having already insisted that its first verse ("Sit at my right hand . . . ") refers to the Son (1:13), the homilist assumes that in verse 4 God continues to speak to the Son:

> *The Lord has sworn and will not change his mind, "you are a priest forever after the order of Melchizedek."*

Since God said Christ is a Melchizedekian priest, the Genesis story and the Psalm can illumine each other. This enables the homilist to exhibit the superiority of Christ's priesthood over that of the Levitical system and to infer that Christ brought the new covenant that God promised in Scripture. Noting some of the homilist's exegetical moves suffices here.

Both priesthoods are unending, but Christ's is grounded in what God said, whereas Melchizedek's is inferred from what Scripture does *not* say: Its silence about his parents implies that he had none, but "*resembling the Son of God* he continues a priest forever" (7:3). The italicized words are basic to the argument because Melchizedek resembles Christ (not the reverse), he foreshadows Christ. *Next*, using the conventions of a hierarchical society, the homilist sees the superiority of Christ's priesthood foreshadowed in the transaction between the two figures in Genesis 14: because Levi (the ancestor of the Levitical priests) was in Abraham's loins, so to speak, Melchizedek's blessing Abraham (his inferior) and Abraham's giving a tithe to Melchizedek (his superior) prefigured the superiority of Christ's priesthood (7:4–10). *Further*, whereas the Levitical priesthood was based on physical descent, Christ became priest by "the power of an indestructible life" (resurrection, 7:16).

Especially important, in declaring Christ to be priest forever, God "swore an oath" (as Psalm 110:4 says), something not said of other priests (7:20–21). According to 6:13–18, God's oath to Abraham shows that "it is impossible that God should prove false." Moreover, in becoming a priest by God's oath, "Jesus has become the guarantor of a better covenant" (7:22), as well. Indeed, Christ is the "mediator" of the new covenant (9:15) that God promised in Jeremiah 31 (quoted at length in 8:8–12). The promise itself implies a critique of the inherited covenant: "If the first had been flawless, there would have been no need of a second" (8:7). As noted above, the old economy of salvation was inherently flawed because it used animal blood in a humanly constructed sanctuary on earth. Even so, it was not wrong, but it was provisional—instituted by God "until the time comes to set things right" (9:10)—that is, until Christ became the eternal priest who offered his own blood.

Christian Life as Journey to God

Given the homily's pastoral purpose, the anthropological/soteriological correlates of its Christology must explain both how the Christ event deals definitively with the human condition and how that event affects the believers' current situation. Hebrews views that situation as a journey toward a goal whose nature is made certain by the *ephapax* character of the Christ event but whose attainment is contingent on the travelers' perseverance. Though their hearts have been "sprinkled clean from an evil conscience" (10:23), they are warned, "Look out . . . lest there be in any of you an evil faithless heart that falls away from the living God" (3:12).

This contingency is expressed by a crucial "if" in statements. For example, in 3:6, believers are Christ's "house" (extended family) "*if* [they] hold firm the confidence and the pride that belongs to hope." This is paraphrased in 3:14: "We have come to share in Christ, if we hold firmly to the very end the confidence we had at first." Otherwise, they will repeat the fate of ancient Israel, whose wilderness rebellion prompted God to swear, "they will not enter my rest" (the end of wandering), as Psalm 95:7–11 says (referring to Exodus 17:1–7; Numbers 20:2–5).[20] In this way the homily interprets the "not yet" of complete salvation as its *current contingency*. Consequently, reaching the journey's ultimate goal—full redemption—depends on both the "when" of God's completing act and the "whether" of the traveler's fidelity.

During the journey, the believers enjoy a new confidence or boldness generated by salvation's "already" and sustained by a distinct understanding of faith. The Greek word for this confidence was *parrēsia*, "the quality of those who speak openly with their superiors," as Thompson puts it. For Philo, the word characterizes speech to God when one is "pure from sin" and free from the judgments of conscience (Thompson, *Hebrews* 105). Likewise, in Hebrews this boldness refers to the believers' audacity before God: "Let us . . . approach the throne of grace with boldness so that we may receive mercy and find grace to help in time of need" (4:16). That this boldness is generated by salvation's "already" is clear in 10:19–22: "Since we have confidence to enter the sanctuary [God's presence] by the blood of Jesus, by the new and living way that he opened for us . . . and since we have a great high priest over the house of God, let us approach with a true heart in the full assurance of faith."

Hebrews may well imply that the believers' confidence is also a sign of their liberation from lifelong fear of death. In any case, according to 5:7–9 Jesus himself manifested such boldness: "In the days of his flesh, Jesus offered up prayer and supplications, with loud cries and fears to the one who was able to save him from death,[21] and was heard because of his reverent submission." (NIV). Jesus did not ask to be spared dying but to be saved out of death; his entreaties were heard because they expressed his *eulabeia* (godly fear, reverent awe). Since *eulabeia* characterizes worship that is acceptable to God (12:28), and since "loud cries and tears" were deemed appropriate traits of serious prayer, Jesus's praying shows his confidence and makes him the prototype of the believers as well (12:1–2).

An especially significant factor in the journey is faith (*pistis*). Having quoted Habakkuk 2:3–4 in which God says, "My righteous one will live by faith" (10:32–39), the homilist provides the New Testament's only definition of faith: "Faith is the assurance of things hoped for, the conviction of things not seen" (11:1)—alluding to the two aspects of the homily's conceptual world. Faith, as here defined, energizes bold action and confident endurance, as the rest of the chapter shows.

But the deeper significance of this definition emerges in what the chapter says about two groups of eminent biblical figures. The antediluvians and patriarchs "died in faith *without* having received the promises." In fact, "they confessed that they were strangers and foreigners on the earth . . . they were seeking a homeland . . . a better country, that is, a heavenly one" (11:13–16). Likewise, the group from Moses to the prophets lived "by faith" and so not only "conquered kingdoms, administered justice," etc., but also endured tortures, "refusing to accept release, in order to obtain a better resurrection." They too "wandered in deserts and mountains." Despite their achievements, enabled "by faith," none of them received the promise either—not because their deeds were flawed, but because "God had planned something better for us so that only together with us would they be made perfect" (11:17–40, NIV).

The definition of faith accounts for three features of this chapter, famous for its oft-repeated "by faith" that made it more effective rhetorically when spoken aloud than when read silently. *First*, receiving God's approval/commendation (11:4, 5, 30) for faith-generated deeds is sharply distinguished from receiving the promise. *Second*, the readers are never urged to emulate either the faith or the achievements of these heroic figures. As a result, the ancients are predecessors, not prototypes. They show what living "by faith" can be like. *Third*, although the celebrated deeds varied greatly—from Abel's more acceptable sacrifice to the unnamed who were sawn in two (11:4, 37)—all were generated "by faith," as defined here.

The definition also underlies what the chapter's last clause assumes: that there is one people of God, constituted by their faith, not determined by physical descent, geography, social status, or cultural heritage. The solidarity of all who now live "by faith" also implies that all are "made perfect" together at the end: all will share in the "something better" that God has in store (11:40) through Christ for the biblical heroes. Jesus is the pioneer and perfecter of this faith since he, too, did not receive the promise in this life, but "endured the cross, disregarding its shame, his eye on the joy set before him" in God's presence. So, then, "consider him who endured such hostility against himself, so that you may not grow weary or lose heart" (12:2–3).

Finally, the homilist insists that in a hostile world, the readers must understand their painful experiences as God's discipline (*paideia*) as Proverbs 3:11–12 says, "My child [literally, son], do not regard lightly the discipline of the Lord . . . the Lord disciplines those whom he loves" (quoted more fully in 12:5–6). Through sufferings, "God [the Father of spirits in verse 9] is treating you as his children," not as illegitimate offspring. Indeed, "what child is there whom the parent does not discipline" (i.e., train rigorously)? Whereas parents discipline us briefly for "our good," God disciplines for a better purpose: "that we may share his holiness" (12:7–11), the equivalent of being perfected.[22]

Although the believers' journey is depicted as perilous and sometimes painful, the travelers' situation is markedly different and better than the Israelites' at Sinai who were terrified by the signs of God's presence (see Exodus 19:16–22, 20:18–21; Deuteronomy 4:11–12, 5:22–23). They came to the touchable mountain they were forbidden to touch, "but you have come to Mount Zion and to the city of the living God [the city sought by Abraham, 11:10], the heavenly Jerusalem, and to innumerable angels in festal gathering, and to the assembly [*ekklesia*] of the first born who are enrolled in heaven, and to God the judge of all, and to the spirits of the righteous made perfect, and to Jesus, the mediator of a new covenant and to the sprinkled blood [of Jesus] that speaks a better word than the blood of Abel" (alluding to 11:4, which implies that Abel's blood, though innocent, was not redemptive). These remarkable lines do not assert that the believers have arrived at journey's end. Rather, their totally positive experience at "Zion" serves a hortatory purpose: the consequences of abandoning this revelation are all the more disastrous (12:25). Exhortations for the lifestyle appropriate for the journey conclude the homily.

The Theological Correlate

In Hebrews this correlate has three components, each reflecting the homily's pastoral concern: the Son's inherent, preexistent relation to God; the perfecting of the earthly Son by God's *paideia*; and the Son's priesthood by divine decree (already mentioned). Together, they assure the disheartened readers that their faith is solidly grounded in a reality that is true and permanent.

The Son: God's Radiance
The homily announces Christ's *innate identity* at the very outset, first by stating what God did with respect to the Son, then by saying who

he is inherently—"the radiance of God's being"—as well as what the Son does: "sustaining all things by his powerful word" (1:2–3, my translation). Seldom do so few words convey so much Christology.[23]

The Son's innate being (or "nature") is formulated by two nouns: He is God's *apaugasma* (radiance, not NRSV's "reflection") and God's *charaktēr* (exact imprint). What is radiated is presumed to be the inherently inseparable, though distinguishable, expression or outward manifestation of its origin. The word *charaktēr*, on the other hand, reflects the making of coins: The well-delivered hammer puts its exact image on the soft metal. With these words, Hebrews claims that the Son is the externalized expression of who God is, as well as evidence of what God is like. Together, these two nouns articulate vividly what the word "divinity" of Christ says more abstractly.

Two verbs state God's two actions pertaining to the Son's role: God "appointed/installed (*ethēken*) him heir of all things" and "created (*epoiēsen*) the worlds "through him." As designated "heir" who inherits everything, he is virtually God's equal; as the one through whom God created the universe (*aeons*, time-space), he is God's agent, the means by which the eternal made the temporal.[24] A single participial phrase (*pherōn ta panta*, "sustaining all things") states the Son's continuing role in the universe he made.

With such statements, but without additional metaphysical explanations, Hebrews, like the rest of the New Testament, maintains that the Son is neither God's competitor nor humanity's rescuer from an evil universe.[25] He is rather the savior of those he himself brought into being. Even so, creation as such is not to be taken for granted; indeed, "by faith we understand that the universe was formed at God's command (*rhēmati*, speech, alluding to Genesis 1), so that what is seen has not been made out of what is visible" (11:3, NIV). (Mentioning the Son's role here was not necessary and would have been a distraction.) In other words, literally, the phenomenal was not shaped out of existing mass but created absolutely (later formulated as created from nothing, *ex nihilo*).

Clearly, summarized in these lines is the Son's inherent identity as a preexisting reality before becoming the Nazarene Jesus. In
Hebrews' three-phased Christ event, the preexistent is the sustainer of
the creation but not the savior of sinful humans. That role requires the
full humanization of the preexistent Son. The homilist can use different language for the same idea, thereby challenging the reader to think
coherently about the subject matter. In short, Hebrews has more than
one way of referring to God's relation to the Christ event.

To begin with, the homily never says that the Son "became" Jesus
(the way John says the Logos "became" flesh). Indeed, "became" may
be the wrong word for Hebrews since it says the Son "was made" like
all humans (2:17; the passive implies that God was the doer). On the
other hand, 10:5 can simply say "when Christ came into the world";
in 9:26, "appeared" is sufficient.

More important, Hebrews not only lacks a birth narrative to
indicate Jesus's true identity but also forgoes viewing his mission as
Spirt-empowered; 9:14 does, however, say he offered himself "through
the eternal Sprit." In Hebrews "the gifts of the Holy Spirit" are given
to believers (2:4); exactly what enabled Jesus to "declare" the word of
salvation did not need to be said. What did need saying, however, is
God's role in fashioning the Son-made-human to be the effective and
compassionate priest.

Perfecting the Son
Hebrews 2:10–13 and 2:17–18 emphasize and explain God's action
in the Christ event. According to the former, it was appropriate that,
in bringing people to the divine presence (here, "glory"), God "should
make the pioneer of their salvation perfect through sufferings." This
way of making the Savior fit for purpose was appropriate because the
sanctifier [Christ] and the sanctified share the same origin (literally "are
from one"; NIV: "of the same family"; NRSV: have "one Father"). That
is, were God's treatment of the Savior different from that of the saved,
Jesus could not be the "pioneer" of *their* salvation.[26] According to the

latter passage, Christ "had to be made like humans" (by God's action) so that he could be the high priest who is both "faithful" to God in making an atoning sacrifice and helpful to tested believers because he himself had been tested. In short, what God did in the incarnation affected both the Son and sinful humans. Had God not acted this way, the Son's arrival in history as Jesus might have been spectacular, but it would not have been salvific. In other words, just as this Christology would not "work" without the solidarity of the Savior and the saved (as noted above), so it would not "work" without God's active participation in the Christ event. Absent such participation, the resulting "Jesus event" would resemble Moses who was faithful in God's house as a servant; Jesus, on the other hand, was faithful *over* the house as a Son (3:1–6). A "Jesus event" would convey quite different "benefits" and generate a different Christology (a "Jesuology") to account for them.

Priest by Decree

Since Jesus did not belong to the priestly tribe, he did not receive his priesthood passively by physical descent, nor did he acquire it assertively by volunteering to serve (thereby glorifying himself, as 5:5 notes). Rather, God "appointed" him to this role by declaration: "You are a priest forever, according to the order of Melchizedek" (5:1–6, 7:16–28). Likewise, it was by divine declaration that he came to be seated at God's right hand, while God was subjecting everything to him (1:13, 2:5, quoting Psalm 110). Moreover, the validity of these declarations is guaranteed by God's oath (7:20–22; see above).

This emphasis on God's declarations, though created by biblical quotations, should neither be taken for granted nor dismissed as artificial. Christologically, it implies that while God's relation to the preexistent Son is an inherent "given" (because the Son is God's *apaugasma*), God's interactions with the Son "in the days of his flesh" (5:7) were deliberate, neither arbitrary nor accidental, but the Father's response to the Son's obedience (see 10:7). Moreover, God "heard" Jesus's fervent prayers "because of his reverent submission" (5:7). In fact, "although he was a Son, he learned obedience [to God] by what he suffered" from humans, and so was "made perfect" by God (5:8–9). Further, God's relation to Jesus, the postexistent permanent priest, assures believers that "he always lives to make intersession for them" (7:25). What the Son experienced on earth enabled him to speak for believers in heaven, always.

Like the Gospels according to Matthew and John, as well as the letter to Christians in Rome, Hebrews teaches us how to think theologically and pastorally about the event bearing the personal name "Jesus."

AFTERWORD

Richard B. Hays

In May 2022, while in New Haven for my undergraduate class reunion, I took one afternoon to pay a visit to Leander Keck. He had been my most influential teacher during my doctoral studies at Emory, and later, after he became Dean of Yale Divinity School, he hired me to my first junior faculty position. Though he had been my inspiration and mentor in the early years of my scholarly career, time and change had intervened; I had not seen him in person for too long a time.

I found him at the age of 94 as sharp, witty, and gracious as ever, despite a number of health challenges. As he explains in the preface of the present book, he had suffered a stroke three years earlier and then survived an exhausting battle with Covid-19. As I commiserated with him, he sighed and lamented, "The thing that frustrates me most is that the stroke has affected my eyesight, so I haven't been able to finish my Christology book."

At that, I laughed out loud and said, "Lee, you've been telling me that for the past thirty years!" I have a clear memory of sitting next to Lee on a bus at the SNTS meeting in Madrid in 1992 and hearing the same lament that he hadn't been able to finish his Christology book. He had, by that time, already been working on it for years—at least since his programmatic paper, "Toward the Renewal of New Testament Christology," at the Trondheim SNTS in 1985. But now, Lee didn't join me in chuckling about his reprise of the same old doleful refrain. Instead, he protested, "But I actually have a complete manuscript! I was just starting the final editing and completion of footnotes before the stroke."

I snapped to attention: "You have a complete manuscript?"

"Yes, and David [his son], is trying to help me get it into shape."

With that, the conversation turned serious. I learned that back in 1990 he actually had signed a contract with Fortress Press to publish the book. I asked, "Lee, would you be willing for me to contact Carey Newman at Fortress about this? I think he would be eager to work with you on getting it into print." He assented, and so began the process that has resulted in the important book now in your hands.

Surveying the Book's Achievement

In this Afterword, my task is to articulate something of the distinctive significance of *Renewing New Testament Christology* for the field of New Testament studies, and to suggest ways that it might point forward for others to continue on the path that it illumines.

The book falls into two distinct sections of equal importance: (1) an exposition and critique of the history of the discipline of New Testament Christology, followed by Keck's own constructive proposal for the redirection of the field; (2) a series of four studies that exemplify what it would mean in practice to treat Christology as "a historically informed *theological* discourse," tracing the logic and reasoning embodied in the four very different Christologies of Matthew, Paul (in Romans), John, and Hebrews. Each of the book's two parts offers rich and provocative food for reflection.

First: the contribution and challenge of the opening section (the historical survey and methodological proposal).

One of the things that Lee Keck always impressed upon his doctoral students was the importance of learning the history of our own discipline. And he insisted that to understand the history of New Testament studies, we must not see it in a vacuum—as though it were a self-contained pipeline of ever-advancing pure research. Instead, we must understand how the evolution of the field has taken place within the broader context of intellectual and cultural history.[1] We need to recognize the ways in which NT scholarship has been influenced and shaped by the questions, concerns, and values of its social environment.

Accordingly, in his opening chapter, Keck sketches the historical process whereby, from the nineteenth century to the present, the previously theological study of Christology morphed into "a history of ideas about Christ," seeking to recover the historical events that gave rise to such ideas, along with the pretextual sources and influences that contributed to their production. While acknowledging certain contributions of this historical project, Keck regards it as a wrong turn that has in significant ways occluded the Christological logic and testimony of the texts themselves: as he puts it, "the history of beliefs replaced the logic of belief, thereby abandoning Christology."[2]

Chapter 1, then, is a learned and incisive distillation of the trajectory of NT studies from Wrede onward, demonstrating how the turn to "history" was driven partly by apologetic concerns—both for conservative traditionalists and for liberal apologists—in the face of modernity's emergent historical consciousness and growing hostility toward Christian faith, exemplified above all by Nietzsche. Keck's account shows how the formulation of Christology as a historical field of study shifted emphasis toward genetic and developmental issues (sources, influences, parallels in ancient religious and philosophical traditions) and away from understanding how the texts actually *work* in articulating the significance of Jesus. Keck's discerning judgments and thought-provoking turns of phrase open windows that let in fresh air and shed new light on many of our settled ways of formulating questions. As a survey of this disciplinary history, this chapter is pure gold; it should be required reading for all serious students of the NT—and not only beginning students.

Chapter 2 then sets forth Keck's own methodological proposal for renewing "a grasp of Christology as such, of what any Christology does and why it does it at all."[3] Particularly salient is Keck's insistence that Christology is necessarily linked to soteriology, and that there is always a reciprocity between the two, because "the cure must fit the disease." Here is his concise articulation of that point:

> *Christology does more than praise Jesus with a special*
> *vocabulary; it also claims that who he was and what he did*
> *deals decisively with the human condition, however that is*
> *diagnosed.*[4]

(I remember well that Lee's emphasis on this point was a recurrent theme in his NT seminars back in the late 1970s.) Accordingly, in the present book, Keck articulates carefully how each of the Christologies that he explicates presupposes a particular diagnosis of the human predicament. Further, he also outlines the way in which any portrayal of Jesus as savior entails an account both of his embodied humanity and of his mysterious relationship to—or identity with—God. The task of Christology, then, is to explore the way in which each NT writing conceives and explicates the human condition, as well as the way in which it correlates the identity of Jesus with both human need and divine saving power.

The answers to such programmatic questions cannot be found through attempting to excavate the Jesus of history; they can be found only through close attention to the logic, both explicit and implicit, of the testimony of the NT texts themselves: "New Testament Christology is the Christology of the New Testament writings. Full stop."[5]

And so, the opening chapters of Keck's book forcefully challenge the direction of "New Testament Christology" as practiced in the scholarly guild for the past 200 years (or so) and draw clear methodological guidelines for a different approach. It remains, then, for him to illustrate this different approach through exposition of the texts themselves; that is what the second part of the book offers us.

It would be superfluous for me to attempt a summary of Keck's fresh and penetrating analyses of the Christologies of Matthew, Romans, John, and Hebrews. I need only say that readers should expect to be surprised, provoked, and stimulated by the close readings found in these chapters. They exemplify qualities that anyone who was privileged to have heard Lee lecture will recognize at once: intellectual gravitas expressed in lively prose full of arresting, witty language that sometimes catches us by surprise and makes us stop and ponder.

Particularly striking to me as I read these chapters was how often Keck forces us to consider what is *not* said in each of these texts.[6] Those of us whose minds have been conditioned by the canon as a whole, and by the larger narrative embodied in the church's liturgical and homiletical traditions, have a habit of harmonizing the texts and filling in the gaps, more or less subconsciously and reflexively. In effect, Keck asks us to stop that. He invites us to join him in considering what each of these audacious writings, taken individually, actually does and does not say about Jesus and how his life, death, and resurrection address our human need.

Where Do We Go from Here?

Renewing New Testament Christology ends abruptly. (Like the Gospel of Mark?) It lacks a concluding summary chapter that might tie the ends together or yield some sort of synthesis. It lacks a programmatic exhortation that would advise NT scholars what to do next after absorbing the message of the book. It just stops. And yet, in that momentous conversation in New Haven last May, Lee described his work to me as "a complete manuscript." He expressed no regrets that he hadn't completely surveyed the Christologies of all the NT writings, no regrets that he hadn't written a conclusion. He seemed to regard this manuscript as the fulfillment of what he had set out to do more than 30 years ago.

What then are we as readers of this book to do? First of all, we should thank Leander Keck for forcing us to stop and reconsider the ways we have thought about the NT and about the hermeneutical models we bring to it—whether those are the preacher's theological convictions or the scholar's methodological conventions. Whatever else

Keck's book does, it calls us to listen carefully to the *testimony* of each individual writing about the significance of Jesus. These testimonies can neither be conflated nor explained away as products of their historical antecedents. They make bold claims that call for our attention and response.

Having said that, there is more here for NT scholars to ponder. Interestingly, Keck declares in his preface that his four chapters on Matthew, Romans, John, and Hebrews could be "read in any sequence because their order is not part of the argument."[7] Certainly, this permission to reshuffle the order of the chapters precludes any temptation to treat them chronologically as an account of the historical development of early Christology. Instead, as Keck advises, "Simply juxtaposing these chapters allows each text to be heard in its own register." Fair enough.

Still, we may ask, why does Keck single out *these* four texts? They are all admittedly major NT witnesses, but what about Mark, Luke (or Luke-Acts), 1 Peter, and Revelation? For that matter, what about the other Pauline letters? Texts such as 1-2 Corinthians, Galatians, Philippians, Colossians, and Ephesians certainly have a good deal to say about Jesus Christ and his significance for the human condition. Presumably, other readers could take Keck's work as an invitation to undertake similar explorations of the Christological logic of these texts. Professor Keck has not given us that assignment, but perhaps appreciative readers could take it upon themselves to carry forward the project on other significant canonical witnesses.

Would an analysis of the Christologies of these other texts align with the texts Keck has explicated so penetratingly? Or not? If not, what shall make of that? Indeed, even considering only the four witnesses that Keck has chosen to write about, what are we to make of their striking diversity? Is there any way to perceive a theological unity in their testimonies about Jesus? Here again, that is a question that Keck has forsworn in his Preface, where he offers this tantalizing observation about his own work:

Part Two shuns talking of NT Christology's "unity" (sometimes
a mischievous word) without thereby doubting that the NT's
diverse Christologies also share certain ways of thinking,
expressed in differing words. Showing this, however, is not this
book's task.[8]

Again, fair enough. No one book can do everything. Still, if our
aim is to understand "NT Christology" theologically, can the synthetic
question of unity in diversity be endlessly deferred? Can we faithfully
describe the "certain ways of thinking" that the texts share? Or is there
at least some way to identify "families" of Christological thinking
within and among the canonical texts? It seems to me that Keck's work,
though he "shuns" such questions for himself, irresistibly invites others
to take them up.

At still another level, might it be useful to explore how the
Christologies of Matthew, Romans, John, and Hebrews relate to
the church's later dogmatic traditions? It is noteworthy that Keck's
readings of these texts consistently affirm the soteriological significance of Christ's preexistence, resurrection, and eschatological
triumph. Likewise, his analysis of the "theological correlate" and
"anthropological/soteriological correlate" in the Christologies of
these texts suggests a necessary emphasis on what the later tradition
would call Jesus Christ's "two natures," both divine and human.
It appears to me that Keck's program of pursuing NT Christology
as a historically informed *theological* discipline might appropri-
ately invite systematic theologians and historians of doctrine to the
table as reading partners.[9] I think Lee Keck would welcome that
conversation.

My point is that Keck's project of *Renewing New Testament
Christology* opens up the field for academic disciplines too long
estranged to come together once again in fruitful conversation about
the complexity of Christology—while still insisting that NT scholarship in its own right has much to contribute to the dialogue.

In this book, Lee Keck has at last offered us the fruits—or better yet, the distillation—of a lifetime of learning. The long deferral of the book's publication has only deepened its savor and its value, like the aging of fine wine. As at Cana, we readers are guests at the feast, grateful guests who are unexpectedly receiving the best wine last. Reader, drink deeply.

Richard B. Hays
December 11, 2022

NOTES

Preface

1 This approach seemed self-evident, having used it in my Yale dissertation: *The Sojourn of the Savior: The Use of the Life of Jesus in Christian Gnosticism,* 1957.

2 In retrospect, important were generating the eight-volume "Lives of Jesus" series that Fortress Press began publishing in 1970 (it included my translation of D.F. Strauss's *The Christ of Faith and the Jesus of History*), as well as writing *A Future for the Historical Jesus* (1971); the first Fortress Press edition of 1981 was reprinted in 2007; Baird's *History of New Testament Research III* (622–40 discusses it fully), *Paul and His Letters* (1979, expanded in 1988), *Who is Jesus?* (2000), and a commentary on *Romans* (2005).

3 Published in the Society's journal, *New Testament Studies* (1982), included in my essays, *Why Christ Matters* (2015).

Chapter 1

1 *Über Aufgabe und Methode der sogenannten neutestamentlichen Theologie* was published promptly but not translated until 1973 as "The Task and Method of New Testament Theology" in Morgan's *The Nature of New Testament Theology*, which also includes his translation of Adolf Schlatter's essay on the same subject, as well as an excellent introduction to both works. Page numbers here refer to the Morgan volume.

2 The third edition was translated and published by T. & T. Clark in Edinburgh in 1882. It had five parts in chronological order: The Teaching of Jesus, The Apostolic Teaching Before Paul, Paulinism (four sections in 13 chapters), The Early Apostolic System in the Post-Pauline Period, and The Johannine Theology. For

a discussion of Weiss's influential work, see Baird, *History* II 101–11.

3 By adding "and theology," Wrede acknowledged that ideas were important in the early Christian religion, though they were not "doctrine," which appears "when thoughts and ideas are developed for the sake of teaching" (75)—that is, as *Lehrbegriffen* (literally, didactic concepts).

4 Wrede was not hostile to the church. In 1892 he addressed the "Scientific Preachers' Society" in Hanover on "The Preacher and his Hearers," drawing on his own experience. In two lectures to theological students in Breslau he showed concern for the impact of biblical criticism on their faith. (These lectures, included in *Vorträge und Studien*, were published posthumously by his brother Adolf in 1907, and are now included in Zager's *William Wrede*.) Even so, in 1893 he declined to address pastors on the dogmatic significance of the life of Jesus, though claiming to have also "a positive stance toward Jesus." (The latter is included in Zager's *Liberale Exegese* 36–39.)

5 The concluding phrase, *wirklich gewesen ist*, virtually repeats Leopold von Ranke's *wie es eigentlich gewesen* [ist], which epitomized his view of scientific historiography.

6 As a vacation course in 1894 Wrede had given three lectures titled, "The Preaching of Jesus about the Kingdom of God"; his 1897 lectures on New Testament theology do not mention them, perhaps because they were not published until 1907 (by his brother), together with public lectures on "Jesus as Son of David" and "Judas Iscariot in Early Christian Tradition." Wrede's *The Messianic Secret* (1901, ET 1971) was a turning point in the Life of Jesus industry, for he undermined confidence in the historical reliability of the Markan outline of Jesus's public life and thought. For an overview of Wrede on Jesus, see Rollmann, "William Wrede, Albert Eichhorn, and the 'Old Quest' of the Historical Jesus," as well as W. Baird, *History* II 144–49.

7 For the 1902 meeting of "The Evangelical Conference in Silesia" Wrede prepared a lecture, "The Character and Tendency of the Gospel of John," but it was read by someone else because Wrede was ill. His brother included it in the collection of essays published in 1907; it can be found now in Zager, *William Wrede*.

8 For an overview of Bousset's work, see Baird, *History* II 243–51. His close friendship with Ernst Troeltsch began in 1884 when both were theological students in Erlangen, and was continued in Göttingen, where they later became faculty colleagues for a time. Both were founders of the "History of Religion School" (discussed below). Upon Bousset's death, Troeltsch reflected on Bousset's role in the group. See "Die kleine Göttinger Fakultät von 1890." Some of Troeltsch's letters to Bousset, written 1894–1914, were published by Erika Dinkler-von Schubert in vol. 20 of the *Heidelberger Jahrbücher*.

9 In 1895 he published a study of the Antichrist traditions in Judaism and Christianity (ET: *The Antichrist Legend*), followed by a commentary on the Book of Revelation (1896). In 1903 came a major study of Judaism in the New Testament era, and a monograph on the history of religion background of Jewish apocalyptic; in 1907 his study of Gnosticism appeared, *Hauptprobleme der Gnosis*.

10 See Hurtado, "New Testament Christology: A Critique of Bousset's Influence," as well as Boers, "Jesus and the Christian Faith: New Testament Christology since Bousset's *Kyrios Christos*." For a survey of the criticisms leveled by Bousset's contemporaries, see Verheule, *Wilhelm Bousset*, 352–65. Hurtado's *Lord Jesus Christ: Devotion to Jesus in Earliest Christianity* is a deliberate attempt to update Bousset's book.

11 See Glawe's exhaustive research in his exhausting book, *Die Hellenisierung des Christentums*, 1912.

12 *History of Dogma* I 143. The first edition appeared in 1885. The quotations are from the translated third edition of 1893, reprinted in 1905.

13 Harnack's famous lectures of 1899–1900, known in English as *What is Christianity?* express the same views (see, e.g., 200, 205, 226). See also Bousset's review of the lectures, "Das Wesen des Christentums."

14 His *Evolution of Christianity* (1914) affirmed the approach but rejected the centrality of the *kyrios* cult; Arthur Darby Nock's "Early Gentile Christianity and its Hellenistic Background" (1928) judged Bousset's claims to generally exceed the evidence.

15 See his *The Origin of Paul's Religion* (1925); Machen had studied with Bousset in 1906.

16 See his "Urchristentum und Religionsgeschichte" (1924). For an appreciative discussion of Holl's wider impact, see Wilhelm Pauck, "Karl Holl."

17 For details, see Drescher, *Ernst Troeltsch* 86–87.

18 For various meanings of "Christendom," see Baumer, "The Concept of Christendom." Butterfield claimed that "modern internationalism is the system of medieval Christendom with the religion evaporated out of it"; *Christianity in European History* 39.

19 See *The Decline of Christendom in Western Europe, 1750–2000*, McLeod and Ustorf, eds., and especially Charles Taylor's comprehensive *A Secular Age*.

20 The word "secular" was first used in this sense by a "free-thinker" George J. Holyoake in 1842 (so Edwards, *Christian England* 295). Owen Chadwick notes that the current understanding was "invented by the social sciences," not by historians. *The Secularization of the European Mind* 5. For the changed roles of the Christian religion, see, Callum G. Brown, *Religion and Society in Scotland Since 1707* as well as his *Religion and Society in Twentieth-Century Britain* and his important essay on methodological problems, "The Secularization Decade: What the 1960s Have Done to the Study of Religious History" in McLeod and Ustorf, *Decline* 29–46. Also worth reading is Gilbert, *The Making of Post-Christian Britain*. For a critical assessment of C. Brown, and of the "secularization" literature, see Morris, "The Strange Death of Christian Britain." See also Rémond, *Religion and Society in Modern Europe* and Norris & Inglehardt, eds., *Sacred and Secular. Religion and Politics Worldwide*. The story of American Christendom includes issues of "church and state" as well as the Evangelicals' desire to restore "Christian America." At the beginning of the twentieth century, however, the President of Princeton University expressed a more specific hope: that a unified Christendom's faith would be Calvinistic. Marsden, *Understanding Fundamentalism* 234–5.

21 See, for example, Peter Brown, *The Rise of Western Christendom*; Judith Herrin, *The Formation of Christendom (6th–9th Centuries)*; A. Kreider, *The Origins of Christendom in the West*, and Ramsey McMullen, *Christianizing the Roman Empire*. But Jean Delmeau,

who thinks real Christianization occurred in the Reformation and Counter-Reformation, declared, "The God of the Christians was much less alive in the past than has been thought and today he is much less dead than is claimed" (quoted by Wessels, *Europe: Was it Ever Really Christian?*). For a still different view, see Russell, *The Germanization of Early Medieval Christianity*.

22 Hatfield traced this development to the influence of "the Greeks" whose actual views, however, were sanitized and idealized; see his *Aesthetic Paganism in German Literature*.

23 Germans distinguished two kinds of sciences (*Wissenschaften*): the *Naturwissenschaften* (natural sciences) and the *Geisteswissenschaften* (literally, the sciences of mind or spirit), which included philosophy, theology, and history. "Humanities" is a useful approximation. Generally, those who looked to the natural sciences as the model for scientific history emphasized objectivity and often sought the "laws" of history; those who saw history as a *Geisteswissenschaft* emphasized hermeneutics and eschewed history's "laws."

24 See Fuchs, "Conceptions of Scientific History in the Nineteenth-Century West" in Wang and Iggers, *Turning-Points in Historiography*, as well as Gay, *The Bourgeois Experience IV: The Naked Heart*, Chap. 3, "Usable Pasts."

25 Novick's *That Noble Dream* shows, however, how often, and in what ways history was bent to serve sundry purposes.

26 So reports Ankersmit, "Historiography and Postmodernism" 138, who also complains that the current overproduction of "studies" distorts the field by emphasizing interpretation more than the texts themselves.

27 Often misunderstood, the phrase has been used to accuse Ranke of being virtually a proto-positivist, interested only in the factuality of the past; but the phrase means more than *what* happened, for it also connotes something like "what was truly going on in what happened." So also Iggers's and von Moltke's Ranke anthology, *The Theory and Practice of History*, xix–xx. Not only was Ranke's goal a universal history, but he also insisted that history is not "simply an immense aggregate of particular facts" (quoted by Stern, *The Varieties of History*, 59). Iggers's *The German Conception of History* situates Ranke in German historiography from

Herder to the present. For a discussion of Ranke's role in the tension between the science of historical research and the rhetoric of historiography, see Rüsen, "Rhetoric and the Aesthetics of History." Still useful are the discussions of Ranke in Butterfield, *Man on His Past* and in Gooch, *History and Historians in the Nineteenth Century.*

28 Niebuhr was a civil servant of both Denmark and Prussia (ambassador to the Vatican 1816–23), as well as lecturer at the new university of Berlin (1810–16), and after 1823 professor at Bonn. For his impact at Oxford, see Jenkyns, "The Beginnings of Greats [classics], 1800–1872" in *History of the University of Oxford* VI 525–30.

29 For details, see Reill, *The German Enlightenment and the Rise of Historicism*, as well as Howard, *Protestant Theology and the Making of the Modern German University* 105–21; Butterfield notes the importance of the Göttingen library for the tradition of philology there; see *Man on His Past* 39–61. For the professionalization of the professoriate at Oxford, see Engel, *From Clergyman to Don.*

30 See, for example, Iggers's chapter, "The Crisis of the Conventional Conception of 'Scientific History'" in his *New Directions in European Historiography*. Regarding the critical analysis of "sources" as modern historiography's greatest contribution, at Berlin J.G. Droysen (1808–84) insisted that "what is before us for investigation is not past events as such, but partly remnants of them, partly ideas of them." Only if we see this "will we cease to 'naturalize' in history"—that is, treat history as a natural science (quoted in Iggers).

31 The literature is both enormous and diverse. The essays in Veeser, *The New Historicism*, show how even recent literary criticism has claimed to be historicist. Windshuttle's *The Killing of History* offers a pungent rebuttal. On the other hand, Davaney's *Historicism* champions a "pragmatic historicism" in theology.

32 *Die Entstehung des Historismus*; the second edition of 1959 was translated and published in 1972 as *Historicism. The Rise of a New Historical Outlook.*

33 See Morgan, "Ernst Troeltsch and the Dialectical Theology" in Clayton, *Ernst Troeltsch and the Future of Theology.*

34 His "Historical and Dogmatic Method in Theology" was first published as supplementary remarks to an essay by F. Niebergall, "On the Absoluteness of Christianity," which criticized Troeltsch. The English translation of Troeltsch's piece is the lead essay in *Religion in History*, a collection of Troeltsch's articles.

35 "Historical relativism" was a major concern of Troeltsch throughout his career. "Relativism," however, has many meanings and associations. For a thorough discussion, see "The Nature of Troeltsch's Relativism" in Coakley, *Christology without Absolutes*.

36 Even so, Troeltsch's view expresses a pruned Hegelian idealism: "For the believer in religion and ethics, history is orderly sequence in which the essential truth and profundity of the human spirit rises from its transcendent ground."

37 For a useful overview of the history of the academic study of religion see Smart's "Religions. The Study and Classifications of," in *The New Encyclopedia Britannica* (15th ed., 2002); for an important analysis of the same phenomena, see J.Z. Smith, *Drudgery Divine*.

38 To the circle also belonged Albert Eichhorn, Hermann Gunkel, and Johannes Weiss (son of Bernhard Weiss, see above); associated with them were Alfred Rahlfs (future editor of the Septuagint), and later Wilhelm Heitmüller and Hugo Gressmann. All became significant figures in German universities.

39 In 1897 Troeltsch wrote, "Everywhere the basic reality of religion is the same: an underivable, purely positive, again and again experienced contact with the Deity. This unity has its ground in a common dynamism of the human spirit which advances in different ways as the result of the mysterious movement of the divine Spirit in the unconscious depth of the human spirit, which is everywhere the same." See "Christianity in the History of Religion" in his *Religion in History*, 79. In 1909 he emphasized as a given religious a priori—a capacity that "can only be analyzed, not psychologically derived." "On the Question of the Religious A Priori," *Religion in History*, 35. Karl Barth would object strenuously to all such talk.

40 The common translation "history of religions school" is misleading because they were not really historians of major religions. What interested them was the history of religion as such. For an

overview, see Baird, *History* II, as well as Ittel, "Die Hauptgedanken der 'religionsgeschichtliche Schule.'" Unfortunately, neither Klatt's study of Gunkel nor Verheule's of Bousset has been translated; Rollmann has announced himself as Wrede's biographer, but only essays have appeared until now.

41 "The Dogmatics of the History-of-Religions School" in *Religion in History*, 92. The original version was requested by *The American Journal of Theology,* which published it in vol. 17 (1913).

42 The experiential focus was signaled in the title of Gunkel's first book (1888), translated nearly a century later as *The Influence of the Holy Spirit* ("influence" flattens the German *Wirkungen* [effects]). In the 1909 edition, Gunkel wrote that the pneumatic person senses the Spirit experienced as the effects of an alien reality, a power not the "I"—that is, the Spirit is not ontically continuous with the human spirit, as in idealist thought. Gunkel asserted that in the sources there are "absolutely no doctrinal statements regarding the Spirit, though we find a host of descriptions of the Spirit's activities." The English publishing convention of capitalizing the nouns in a book title obscures Gunkel's point: the book is not about the Holy Spirit but about the holy Spirit.

43 *Zum religionsgeschichtliche Verstandnins des Neuen Testaments* 1, 95, resp. For criticisms of Gunkel's use of "syncretism" see Ittel, "Hauptgedanken," 69–70. Other members of the group generally avoided the term while sharing the point of view.

44 Colpe's *Die Religionsgeschichtliche Schule* (1961) concentrates on Reitzenstein in order to assess negatively the way the redeemer myth and the redemption motif were constructed.

45 Gunkel reported that during a lecture tour, the local pastors had agreed to preach against him on the Sunday before he arrived. So Klatt, *Gunkel*, 85.

46 An English version, containing some translations from the fourth edition, is being published by Brill, titled *Religion Past and Present*, beginning 2007.

47 The series, *Religionsgeschichtliche Volksbücher,* had five sections: The Religion of the New Testament, of the Old Testament, General History of Religion, Church History, and Worldviews and Philosophy of Religion. In the first section appeared Bousset's *Jesus* (1904; ET 1907).

48 His *What is Religion?* (1907; German orig. 1903) asserts that since Jesus freed religion "from all national claims . . . from ceremonial, from the letter of the law, and from the domination of erudition" (223–42), Christianity "as a moral religion of redemption stands at the head of all religions" and is "the religion of the progressive nations of the earth"—thereby restating Christendom's self-understanding. His *The Faith of a Modern Protestant* (1908; German orig. 1908) aims to make belief intellectually credible and religiously inspiring.

49 *The Absoluteness of Christianity and the History of Religions* 95, 114–15 (1971). This book translated the third posthumous edition of 1929; the first edition of 1901 expands lectures to a general audience. Page numbers here refer to the 1971 edition.

50 "The Dogmatics of the History-of-Religions School" in *Religion in History* 90–102. Troeltsch's systematic theology, published posthumously in 1925 on the basis of student notes of his onetime lectures of 1912–13, was translated in 1991 as *The Christian Faith*.

51 *The Absoluteness of Christianity*, 123.

52 Marsden notes that "between 1878 and 1906 almost every major denomination experienced at least one heresy trial, usually of a seminary professor." *Understanding Fundamentalism*, 38.

53 Callum Brown enthusiastically claims that this understanding of "history" is the achievement of postmodernism—a label as ambiguous as "secularization." *Postmodernism for Historians*. Be that as it may, Harnack reported that Goethe saw the point long ago when he told a historian, "Not all that is presented to us as history has really happened; and what ready happened did not actually happen the way it is presented to us; moreover, what really happened is only a small part of all that happened." So Pauck, *Harnack and Troeltsch* 20.

54 *Metahistory* 2, his ital. Building on White, Ann Rigney's *Imperfect Histories* suggestively explores what representation of the past entails; see chapter 2.

55 Paul Schubert expressed the point in his customary salty language: "But such is the malice of history that no one can write even the most sterile history of a single decade without making value judgments before he lays hand to pen. Thus the 'purely

objective' historian is the worst of all sinners against history, since he must unknowingly and unwillingly do the very thing he would not do knowingly and willingly." "New Testament Study and Theology," 557.

56 See, for example, Gardner, *The Nature of Historical Explanation* and Passmore, "Explanation" in Nadel, *Studies in The Philosophy of History*, 16–34. Suggestive is White's analysis of the rhetorical strategy historians use to "explain": emplotment (the kind of narrative structure used: romance, tragedy, comedy, or satire), formal argument, or ideological implications (e.g., idealization of a past to be restored); see *Metahistory*, 7–29 for a summary.

57 Here, too, White's observations are pertinent: "Unlike literary fiction, such as the novel, historical works are made up of events that exist outside the consciousness of the writer . . . Unlike the novelist, the historian confronts a veritable chaos of events *already constituted*, out of which he must choose elements of the story he would tell in accord with the kind of story he would write" (*Metahistory* 6 n. 5, his ital.).

58 Frei's *The Eclipse of Biblical Narrative* deals extensively with this reversal.

59 The exaltation of history both in Marxist thought and in the Christian recourse to *Heilsgeschichte* (salvation history) in order to overcome the implications of *Religionsqeschichte* (history of religion) deserves attention, but not here.

60 Immanuel Kant (1724–1804) analyzed religion without positing or denying the existence of God, thereby portraying religion as a purely human phenomenon explainable by relying on reason alone.

61 David Friedrich Strauss (1808–74) coined these contrasting phrases for the title of his book-length review of Schleiermacher's *Life of Jesus* (published posthumously in 1864). English translations of both books appeared in the Lives of Jesus series published by Fortress Press (see the Preface, above). My Introduction to Strauss's review traces his repeated efforts to come to terms with Schleiermacher, beginning with his own 1835 Life of Jesus (and ending with its third edition of 1839); the translated fourth edition, with an Introduction by Peter Hodgson, was also included in the Lives of Jesus series.

62 To be sure, the "Jesus of history" is not wholly Christology-free in everyone's eyes, for many scholars have argued that Jesus did regard himself as the Messiah (though understanding this role in his own way); besides, most critics acknowledge that his sense of mission implied a nascent Christology of some kind.

63 "Jesus and the Christian Faith," 452.

64 "The Historical Jesus and the Theology of the New Testament," 201. Morgan does not mention Boers.

65 As used here, "guise" is neither what is deliberately concealed nor deliberately deceptive; it refers to what nonetheless unintentionally turns out to be not what it claims or intends to be.

66 The charge that Christianity rests on a deception has not died out ever since H. S. Reimarus asserted it in the 18th century. Gerd Lüdemann published *The Great Deception and What Jesus Really Said and Did*; its American edition included a "Letter to Jesus" in which he tells Jesus, "You deceived yourself, and your message has been falsified by your supporters for their own advantage contrary to the historical truth" (4). Except for the accusation of self-deception, Reimarus had said the same things.

67 *What is Religion?* 279–81, ital. added. Conveniently for Bousset, when Jesus said no one is good except God (Mark 10:18), "he made the dogma of Christ's divinity almost impossible." At the University of Chicago, Bouset's contemporary, G.B. Smith, urged, "Let us . . . with truthful moral earnestness interpret the significance of Jesus as the great citizen of this world, who conquered for himself a real companionship with the God who ever toils at the task of making the world better. To declare that 'the religion of Jesus' is not the center of Christianity is to rob the church and the world of its greatest religious asset." "The Religious Significance of The Humanity of Jesus," 208.

Chapter 2

1 For a full discussion of resurrection in postbiblical Jewish thought, see N.T. Wright, *The Resurrection of the Son of God,* chap. 4. A.F. Segal has linked belief in resurrection to the socioeconomic status of those who affirmed the idea; see "Life after Death: The Social Sources" in *The Resurrection,* Stephen Davis, et al., eds., 90–125.

2 The assertion in Acts 4:12 that salvation is to be found only in Jesus offends many who value pluralism in religions, but the previous verses make it clear that the claim is the logical consequence of believing that (only) Jesus is resurrected. Given this conviction, the assertion expresses inevitable audacity, not parochial or imperial arrogance.

3 See Simon Gathercole, *The Pre-existence of Christ in the New Testament*.

4 See also Keck, "The New Testament and Nicea" in *Why Christ Matters,* esp. pp. 142–156.

Chapter 3

1 Most scholars think that the Evangelist—whatever his name—used Mark (written two decades before) and Q (scholars' jargon for a collection of Jesus's sayings, perhaps compiled by 50 CE and used also in Luke but not in Mark). To this he added material found only in Matthew. Matthew's author sometimes repeated these "sources" unchanged, sometimes rearranged their sequence, and sometimes expanded or abbreviated them. Scholars have found such modifications to be important clues for constructing this Gospel's first readers.

2 For various reasons, many Christians are distressed, rightly, by the vituperative tone of Matthew 23, though it is comparable to that found in "The Dead Sea Scrolls" and Greco-Roman literature of the time. See L.T. Johnson, "The New Testament's Anti-Jewish Slander and the Conventions of Ancient Polemic," *JBL*, 108 (1989) 419–41.

3 Current opinion locates Matthew in either an unspecified place in upper Galilee/Syria or in a major center of early Christianity, Antioch. According to Acts 11:19–30, hellenized Jewish believers, fleeing persecution in Jerusalem, brought their version of the Christian faith to this city (probably ca. 35 CE) and soon added gentile believers to their group. Acts also reports that the "disciples" were first called "Christians" (Christ people) in Antioch, but it does not say by whom or whether the word was simply descriptive or an epithet of derision.

4 The word "all" unifies the whole passage: all authority; all the nations/ gentiles, all that Jesus commanded; all the days (until the end).

5 Commentators often see a parallel in ancient rabbinic view of Torah study: "if two sit together and the words of the Law [are spoken] between them, the divine presence [the *Shekinah*] rests between them" (*Pirke Aboth* 3:2). Matthew was written much earlier than this text, but the Evangelist may have known the old idea.

6 There are many additional fulfillment passages: 8:17; 12:17–21; 13:14–15; 13:35; 21:4–5; 26:54, 56; 27:9–10.

7 The reason is obscure until one realizes that behind the Greek *Iēsous* is the Hebrew *Yehoshua*, "God saves."

8 See the discussion in Knowles *Jeremiah in Matthew's Gospel*, 265–89.

9 See especially Allison, *The New Moses* and Knowles, *Jeremiah in Matthew's Gospel*, chap. 4.

10 Emphasizing the gospel as a whole does, however, marginalize (without obviating) both source criticism's quest for the origins of what Matthew reports and redaction criticism's reliance on the ways the Evangelist adapted what he adopted from Mark and Q. Above all, since New Testament Christology is understood here as the Christology of texts, one need not speculate why the Evangelist wrote what he did. What matters here is the result of what he wrote.

11 Only in Matthew does Jesus use the word *ekklēsia* (assembly). In 16:18 he says, "I will build *my ekklēsia*. Later in giving directions for discipline he uses it two more times" (18:17–18). To these NRSV *adds* two others by replacing "brother" with "member of the church" (18:15, 21). The narrator never uses the word, nor does he ever define or describe the *ekklēsia*. That Jesus himself used this Greek word is unlikely; that it translates an Aramaic or Hebrew word that Jesus did use is debated.

12 While Matthew assumed that this forgiveness is sealed in the church's baptism (28:19), it never says that Jesus had baptized or had called for baptism.

13 The reasoning rests on several assumptions: Fathers do not call their male offspring "lord," David wrote this psalm, this "my lord" is David's lord, and David's lord is the messiah. But how can the Lord messiah be David's son?

14 At his arrest, when someone had cut off the ear of the high priest's slave, Jesus rebukes the man, "Do you think that I cannot appeal

to my Father, and he will at once send me more than twelve legions of angels?" (27:54).

15 Comparable assertions of his irreplaceable centrality are made by Jesus in John whose Logos Christology undergirds them ontologically. In Matthew, however, the virgin birth is not said to warrant Jesus's self-confident claims.

16 Since the Evangelist is responsible for everything in Matthew, it does not matter here whether the point is made by the narrator or Jesus. The distinction, if detectable, is of course important in historical investigation.

17 In Luke 3:7–14 John the Baptist insists that true repentance must produce right deeds.

18 The rest of the Isaiah quotation pertains to Jesus's critique of the Pharisees' reliance on oral tradition of Torah: "in vain do they worship me, teaching human precepts as doctrine" (NIV: "their teachings are but rules taught by men").

19 By translating *dikaios* as "innocent" instead of "righteous," NRSV and NIV turn a moral assessment of Jesus into a juridical verdict that preempts what Pilate will say in 27:24. Though some manuscripts say he announced, "I am innocent of this righteous man's blood," most critics regard this "righteous" as an addition to what the Evangelist had written.

20 Only in 9:2–8 does Jesus declare a person's sins forgiven, and his instructions to the dispatched disciples do not mention forgiving sins. Nonetheless, at the Lord's Supper Jesus asserts that his death is "for the forgiveness of sins" (26:28).

21 Chapter 1 should have shown that here "Jesus" is actually the man as imaged and interpreted by Christian tradition, oral or written, not a figure wholly purged of faith's perception and commitment. Indeed, one might well ask whether the Evangelist wrote Matthew partly to counter the notion (and trend?) that one could have direct access to Jesus without the mediating role of tradition—that is, apart from the church's memory.

22 Wilken, *The First Thousand Years*, 13.

23 The passages in which Jesus does use "brothers" to refer to his disciples (12:50, 25:40, 28:10) do not concern their relation to God.

24 The many problems created by the wording of the quotation need not detain this discussion. They can all be pursued in Richard

Beaton's *Isaiah's Christ in Matthew's Gospel*, which also summarizes the vast scholarship devoted to addressing these problems.

25 For a thorough treatment of this possibility see Simon J. Gathercole, *The Pre-existent Son*.

Chapter 5

1 The same "elder" probably wrote both 2 John and 3 John, and perhaps also 1 John, though it is really a homily with different concerns. None of the four writings mentions any of the others, making it hard to know the order in which they were written. Despite their differences in form (gospel, letter, and homily) and content, they are all recognizably "Johannine." The Book of Revelation and the noncanonical Acts of John need not be part of this discussion.

2 Why Jesus loved him is neither explained nor implied. His love of Jesus, however, is shown at the end: he was the only disciple at the crucifixion. It was to him that Jesus entrusted his mother (19:25–27). For an excellent discussion of the problems created by the presence of the Beloved Disciple in John, see Culpepper, *John*, chap. 3.

3 The problem of John's relations to the Synoptics need not detain this discussion. It seems impossible to demonstrate convincingly whether John was created to correct or to displace one of the Synoptics, if indeed the beloved disciple even knew of them (or simply knew what their author also knew), let alone whether Matthew was created to counterweight the influence of John. For such matters, see D. Moody Smith, *John Among the Gospels*.

4 Noteworthy is R.E. Brown's *The Community of the Beloved Disciple*, which posits four stages in the community's history. Brown's work complements J.L. Martyn's *History and Theology in the Fourth Gospel*. Martin Hengel's *The Johannine Question* provides a quite different history.

5 Expulsion from synagogues did not occur during Jesus's lifetime, but is plausible in John's time (in the 90s CE). As noted in the discussion of Matthew, to a prayer used in synagogues, a curse on various heretics (not only Christians) was added ca. 85 CE.

6   The noun *martyria* is sometimes translated as testimony, some-times as witness; its verbal form is rendered as testify or bear witness.

7   Likewise, 4:21 flows smoothly into 4:22–24, and 5:18 into 5:19–47.

8   The subtitle of my book *Who Is Jesus?* "History in Perfect Tense" paraphrases the point.

9   The abrupt shift to the plural "you" here makes the readers also recipients of the promise.

10 Noted are the time of day (1:39), the size as well as the number of jars (2:6); the number of porticoes at the pool (5:2); the abun-dance of grass where the crowd is fed (6:10); the origin of the mud used to cure blindness (9:6); the name of the slave whose ear Peter cut off (18:1); and the number of fish caught (21:11).

11 Each of John's three sections opens with an appropriate incident that signals what is significant in what comes next. Just as mak-ing superior wine from purification water (2:1–11) and expel-ling merchants from the temple (2:13–16) point to the intended import of Jesus's mission among the Jewish people, so the foot-washing (13:1–11) points to his relation to "his own." Likewise, the Jesus portrayed at his arrest (18:1–11) signals his sovereignty at his trials.

12 Calling John's view "sectarian," while suggestive, can also be a mischievous anachronism that limits understanding John in John's terms.

13 The absence of the noun did not stop a second-century Valentin-ian gnostic, Heracleon, from writing the first-known commen-tary on John.

14 John with Leszek Kolakowski's observation: "The Whole Chris-tian philosophical, theological and moral teaching is ultimately about a single question: how is the reality of our worldly expe-rience related to the primordial, creative, infinite divine reality which in the realm of finite things is both manifested and con-cealed?" (*God Owes Us Nothing*, 182; also 189; 192).

15 The Baptizer, too, was "sent" (1:6), but he did not preexist or descend from heaven. This unusual use of the same language for two quite different persons (emphasized in 1:7–9) may reflect the history of Johannine Christology. That is, "sending" might be a

mark of a "low" Christology that regards Jesus as a prophet who speaks for God. The "high" incarnation Christology could then simply absorb it, as in 7:29.

16 In Jesus's exchange with Nicodemus "born of God" is paraphrased as "born *anothen*, from above."

Chapter 6

1 Not until the end does the homilist commend himself: "we are sure that we have a clear conscience, desiring to act honorably in all things" (13:18). What our homilist delays to the end other speakers often put at the beginning.

2 So Dunhill, *Covenant and Sacrifice*, p. 2.

3 *Das Wandernde Gottesvolk*, 10.

4 Other NT writers also used the language of illumination (e.g., Rom 13:12, Eph 5:14, 1 Pet 2:9). "Once" does not mean "sometime" (as in "I once owned a Chevrolet") but qualifies conversion as a one-time, unrepeatable event.

5 Many find the rejection of second repentance to be the most troublesome idea in the whole homily. Fortunately, its Christology can be understood without explaining these passages, though they cannot be understood apart from the Christology.

6 At least since Paul wrote 1 Corinthians 15:25, 27 (early 50s CE) Psalm 110 was taken as referring to Christ's heavenly enthronement; see, for example, Acts 2:34–35, Matthew 22, 4–45, and Revelation 3:21.

7 This Christological interpretation is preferable to the anthropological reading of Hebrews, which retains the Hebrew Bible's celebration of human dignity ("a little lower" than God) and mastery ("dominion" over creation). The homily, however, has no interest whatever in humanity's sovereignty. The Christological reading of Hebrews 2:5–9 assumes that the homilist understands the Greek *brachu* not as "a little lower" as in the Hebrew behind the Greek, but as "a little while," just as he understands the Psalm's "son of man" (human) to mean the Son of Man (not "mortals" as in NRSV).

8 NIV's translation is preferable, for NRSV's "we do not yet see" implies that in due course we will see Christ's universal sovereignty on earth—a view totally foreign to that of Hebrews.

9 Good introductions to Philo are provided by Sandmel, *Philo of Alexandria* and the more recent essays in *The Cambridge Companion to Philo* edited by A. Kamesar; Winston's *Philo of Alexandria* includes important passages.

10 Carlston, "The vocabulary of Perfection in Philo and Hebrews," 148.

11 Two-age language appears repeatedly in Hebrews: "in these last days" (1:4), "at the end of the age" (9:26), "the coming world" (2:5), "the age to come" (6:5). Reflecting apocalyptic thought is the reference to Christ's second coming (8:28), alluded to also in 10:37–38, using language from Isa 26:20 and Hab 2:4 (where the Greek diverges from the Hebrew).

12 Schenk's monograph, *Cosmology and Eschatology in Hebrews,* provides an excellent discussion and often agrees with the position here reached independently.

13 Following Aristotle's *Rhetorica*, ancient rhetoricians distinguished three kinds of speeches: the forensic (aimed at a verdict about the past), the deliberative (leading to a decision about future action), and the epideictic (praise or blame for a person or event). Though some have seen Hebrews as epideictic, it wants the reader to understand Christ's significance, not to praise him.

14 Ancient rhetoricians regraded *logos* (reason, argument, as well as word) as one of three modes of persuasion, along with *ethos* (the speaker's qualifications) and *pathos* (the hearer's emotions). Hebrews uses all three.

15 See Thompson, "The Appropriate, the Necessary, and the Impossible: Faith and Reason in Hebrews" in *The Early Church in its Context*, A. Malherbe et al. eds., Leiden: Brill, 1988.

16 For a useful discussion of the various views of sacrifice in ancient Greek and Jewish religion, see Frances M. Young, *The Use of Sacrificial Ideas in Greek Christian Writers from the New Testament to John Chrysostom*, 7–73.

17 In this terse statement the homilist taps into both the Jewish apocalyptic and the Greco-Roman heritage in order to create something new in the Christology. That the messiah would defeat satanic powers was common in apocalyptic thought. That contemplating one's mortality generated fear of death was said by many Greco-Roman moralists (as commentaries show). Philo

declared, "Nothing is so calculated to enslave the mind as fear of death through a desire to live" (quoted from Johnson, *Hebrews*, 100). But fear of death was not universal, and the Epicureans sought to free people from this fear by redefinition: since the concatenation of atoms that constitute the selfdisintegrates at death, there is no self to experience it. As some put it, there is nothing to fear because where we are, death is not; where death is, we are not. According to the *Targum Neofiti*, Cain, the first murderer, anticipated this view (see Lane, *Hebrews* 2:249–50).

18 Unfortunately, the homily's critique has been read as a denigration of Judaism and a legitimation of Christianity's "supersession." But the homily is not talking about two religions. When Hebrews was probably written, Judaism, not only in the diaspora, was centered in the synagogue (sacrifices in the temple having ended in 70 CE), the base of the rabbinate (neither mentioned nor alluded to in Hebrews). The continuing validity of "Judaism" was not the homilist's problem; his problem was the continuing vitality of the dismayed Christian community. In using both the "Platonic" worldview and Scripture's own criticism of the tabernacle's sacrifices, the homilist sought to show just how preposterous "drifting away" really is. His task was to achieve preserving loyalty to Christ, not to expose the place of "Judaism" and "Christianity" in the history of religion.

19 The homilist was not the only one interested in this obscure figure. A sizable literature has been produced by scholars trying to describe and trace the development of diverse Melchizedek traditions, including the Qumramian 11 Q Melch, and to then relate them to Hebrews. No real influence on Hebrews has been demonstrated; the homilist goes his own way, relying only on Scripture and inference.

20 In Johnson's commentary, "Excursus 2: The Wilderness as Paradigm" summarizes the long history of using the wilderness experience in moral and religious exhortations (119–22).

21 It is unlikely that the homilist refers specifically to the story of Jesus in Gethsemane in Luke 22:39–46. That "who is able . . . death" is a paraphrase for "God" is confirmed by 11:19.

22 The homilist assumes that his readers, too, are familiar with the traditional and widely discussed understanding of *paideia*

as rigorous training that is both moral and physical, sometimes formulated as an untranslatable wordplay: *emathen aph' hōn epathen* (he learned from what he suffered). In 5:8–9 this motif was applied even to Jesus: though a Son he "learned obedience through what he suffered" and so was "perfected."

23 The rest of this opening sentence states Christ's saving work ("purification for sin") and subsequent enthronement, as well as the resulting status (superior to angels, spelled out in the rest of the chapter) and dignity (a superior name, probably "Son," thus "Son" frames the whole Christological paragraph). It is unnecessary, and probably unwarranted, to infer that the homily emphasizes the Son's superiority over angels in order to undermine the readers' improper interest in them.

24 Comparable things are said in John 1:3 about the Logos ("all things came into being through him") about "the Lord Jesus" in 1 Cor 8:16 ("through whom are all things and through whom we exist"), and of God's "beloved Son" in Col 1:16 ("in him all things in heaven and on earth were created . . . all things have been created through him and for him"). That such assertions reflect the influence of ancient Hebrew theology of Wisdom (*Sophia*) has long been recognized. Positing the *Logos* or *Sophia* as God's means of creation spared theologians from saying that the eternal, ineffable deity was directly involved in creating the phenomenal, tangible, palpable, temporal universe.

25 In 2:10 the homily tells the readers that *God* is the one "for whom and *through* whom all things exist," though in 1:2 it said that it was *through the Son* that God created the worlds. Since the Son is God's "radiance," there is no material disparity between these expressions. Besides, both were commonplaces in Stoic thought.

26 To support this argument, 2:11–13 appeals to the three-phased Christ event because it shows that Christ "is not ashamed" to call the saved humans his siblings (literally, brothers). Using Old Testament quotations, Christ refers to phase one as his purpose in coming to humans: "I will proclaim your name to my siblings"; in phase two he states his own relation to God: "I will put my trust in God"; the third quotation refers to the third phase, his and the siblings' arrival in God's presence: "Here am I and the children whom God has given me."

Afterword

1 Keck's concern for placing the discipline of NT studies within a broader intellectual history was exemplified by his spearheading and editorship of the "Lives of Jesus" series in the 1970s.

2 See page 10. It should be highlighted that Keck does not at all reject historical study; indeed, his call for a *historically informed* study of the NT's theological discourse about Jesus presupposes that historical study is both valuable and necessary. He simply does not want historical study (the history of beliefs) to supplant or be confused with *theological interpretation* of the NT's testimony about the saving significance of Jesus (the logic of belief). Understanding the latter is the goal of Keck's work in this book.

3 See page 31.

4 See page 28.

5 See page 46.

6 See the section in chapter 2 on "Fragments and Silences," pages 37–42.

7 See page xxi.

8 See page xxi.

9 For one example of this sort of interdisciplinary conversation, see Beverly Roberts Gaventa and Richard B. Hays, eds., *Seeking the Identity of Jesus: A Pilgimage* (Grand Rapids: Eerdmans, 2008).

WORKS CITED

Allison, Dale C. *The New Moses: A Matthean Typology.* Minneapolis, MN: Fortress Press, 1993.

Ankersmit, Frank R. "Historiography and Postmodernism." *History and Theory* 28, no. 2 (1989): 137–53.

Aston, T. H. *The History of the University of Oxford.* Oxford: Clarendon Press, 1984.

Baird, William. *History of New Testament Research.* Minneapolis, MN: Fortress Press, 1992.

Beaton, Richard. *Isaiah's Christ in Matthew's Gospel.* Cambridge, UK: Cambridge University Press, 2002.

Betz, Hans Dieter. *Religion Past and Present.* [Translation and adaptation of the 4th ed. of *Religion in Geschichte und Gegenwart*]. Leiden: Brill NV, 2012.

Boers, Hendrikus. "Jesus and the Christian Faith: New Testament Christology since Bousset's Kyrios Christos." *Journal of Biblical Literature* 89, no. 4 (1970): 450–56.

Bousset, Wilhelm. *The Antichrist Legend.* London: Hutchinson and Co, 1896.

———. *Hauptprobleme Der Gnosis.* Göttingen: Vandenhoeck und Ruprecht, 1907.

———. *Kyrios Christos: a History of the Belief In Christ From the Beginnings of Christianity to Irenaeus.* Nashville: Abingdon Press, 1970.

———. "Das Wesen des Christentums." *Theologische Rundschau* (1901): 89–103.

Bousset, Wilhelm, and F. B. Low. *The Faith of a Modern Protestant.* New York: C. Scribner's Sons, 1909.

———. *What Is Religion?* London: T. F. Unwin, 1907.

Brown, Callum G. *Postmodernism for Historians.* Harlow, England: Pearson/Longman, 2005.

———. *Religion and Society in Scotland Since 1707.* Edinburgh: Edinburgh University Press, 1997.

———. *Religion and Society In Twentieth-century Britain.* Harlow, UK: Pearson Longman, 2006.

Brown, Peter. *The Rise of Western Christendom: Triumph and Diversity, A.D. 200–1000.* Cambridge, MA: Blackwell, 1996.

Brown, Raymond E. *The Community of the Beloved Disciple.* New York: Paulist Press, 1979.

Butterfield, Herbert. *Christianity In European History.* London: Collins, 1952.

———. *Man On His Past: The Study of the History of Historical Scholarship.* Boston: Beacon Press, 1960.

Carlston, Charles. "The Vocabulary of Perfection in Philo and Hebrews." *Unity and Diversity in New Testament Theology* (1978): 133–60.

Chadwick, Owen. *The Secularization of the European Mind in the Nineteenth Century.* Cambridge: Cambridge University Press, 1990.

Clayton, John Powell. *Ernst Troeltsch and the Future of Theology.* Cambridge: Cambridge University Press, 1976.

Coakley, Sarah. *Christ Without Absolutes: A Study of the Christology of Ernst Troeltsch.* Oxford: Clarendon Press, 1988.

Colpe, Carsten. *Die Religionsgeschichtliche Schule: Darstellung und Kritik Ihres Bildes Vom Gnostischen Erlösermythus.* Göttingen: Vandenhoeck & Ruprecht, 1961.

Culpepper, R. Alan. *John, the Son of Zebedee: The Life of a Legend.* Columbia, SC: University of South Carolina Press, 1994.

Davaney, Sheila Greeve. *Historicism: The Once and Future Challenge for Theology.* Minneapolis: Fortress Press, 2006.

Davis, Stephen T., Daniel Kendall, and Gerald O'Collins. *The Resurrection: An Interdisciplinary Symposium On the Resurrection of Jesus.* Oxford: Oxford University Press, 1997.

Drescher, Hans-Georg. *Ernst Troeltsch: Leben Und Werk.* Göttingen: Vandenhoeck & Ruprecht, 1991.

Dunnill, John. *Covenant and Sacrifice in the Letter to the Hebrews.* Cambridge: Cambridge University Press, 1992.

Edwards, David L. *Christian England.* Grand Rapids, MI: Eerdmans, 1983.

Engel, A. J. *From Clergyman to Don: the Rise of the Academic Profession In Nineteenth-century Oxford.* Oxford: Oxford University Press, 1983.

Frei, Hans W. *The Eclipse of Biblical Narrative: A Study in Eighteenth and Nineteenth Century Hermeneutics.* New Haven: Yale University Press, 1974.

Gardiner, Patrick L. *The Nature of Historical Explanation.* London: Oxford University Press, 1952.

Gathercole, Simon J. *The Preexistent Son: Recovering the Christologies of Matthew, Mark, and Luke.* Grand Rapids, MI: W.B. Eerdmans Pub. Co., 2006.

Gay, Peter. *The Naked Heart.* New York: Norton, 1995.

Gilbert, Alan D. *The Making of Post-Christian Britain: A History of the Secularization of Modern Society.* London: Longman, 1980.

Glawe, Walther. *Die Hellenisierung Des Christentums.* Berlin: Trowitzsch, 1909.

Gooch, G. P. *History and Historians in the Nineteenth Century.* 2nd edition, revised with a new Introduction. London: Longmans, Green, 1952.

Gunkel, Hermann. *The Influence of the Holy Spirit According to the Popular View of the Apostolic Age and the Teaching of the Apostle Paul: A Biblical-theological Study.* Philadelphia: Fortress Press, 1979.

———. *Zum Religionsgeschichtlichen Verständnis Des Neuen Testaments.* Göttingen: Vandenhoeck & Ruprecht, 1903.

Harnack, Adolf von. *History of Dogma.* New York: Dover Publications, 1961.

Harnack, Adolf von, and T. Bailey Saunders. *What Is Christianity?* 1st Fortress Press ed. Philadelphia: Fortress Press, 1986.

Hatfield, Henry Caraway. *Aesthetic Paganism in German Literature: From Winckelmann to the Death of Goethe.* Cambridge: Harvard University Press, 1964.

Hengel, Martin, and John Stephen Bowden. *The Johannine Question.* London: SCM Press, 1989.

Herrin, Judith. *The Formation of Christendom.* Princeton, NJ: Princeton University Press, 1989.

Holl, Karl. *Urchristentum und Religionsgeschichte.* Gütersloh: C. Bertelsmann, 1925.

Howard, Thomas Albert. *Protestant Theology and the Making of the Modern German University.* Oxford: Oxford University Press, 2006.

Hurtado, Larry W. *Lord Jesus Christ: Devotion to Jesus In Earliest Christianity.* Grand Rapids, MI: W.B. Eerdmans, 2003.

———. "New Testament Christology: A Critique of Bousset's Influence." *Theological Studies* 40, no. 2 (1979): 306–17.

Iggers, Georg G. *The German Conception of History: The National Tradition of Historical Thought From Herder to the Present.* Middletown, Conn.: Wesleyan University Press, 1983.

———. *New Directions in European Historiography.* Rev. ed. Middletown, CT: Wesleyan University Press, 1984.

Ittel, Gerhard Wolfgang. "Die Hauptgedanken Der 'Religionsgeschichtlichen Schule' 1." *Zeitschrift für Religions-und Geistesgeschichte* 10, no. 1 (1958): 61–78.

Johnson, Luke Timothy. *Hebrews: A Commentary.* Louisville, KY: Westminster John Knox Press, 2006.

———. "The New Testament's Anti-Jewish Slander and the Conventions of Ancient Polemic." *Journal of Biblical Literature* 108 (1989): 419–41.

Kamesar, Adam. *The Cambridge Companion to Philo.* Cambridge: Cambridge University Press, 2009.

Kant, Immanuel. *Religion within the Limits of Reason Alone.* New York: Harper, 1960.

Käsemann, Ernst. *The Testament of Jesus: A Study of the Gospel of John in the Light of Chapter 17.* Philadelphia: Fortress Press, 1968.

———. *Das Wandernde Gottesvolk: Eine Untersuchung zum Hebräerbrief.* Göttingen: Vandenhoeck & Ruprecht, 1939.

Klatt, Werner. *Hermann Gunkel: zu Seiner Theologie Der Religionageschichte und Zur Entstehung Der Formgeschichtlichen Methode.* Göttingen: Vandenhoeck u. Ruprecht, 1969.

Keck, Leander E. *Christ's First Theologian: The Shape of Paul's Thought.* Waco, TX: Baylor University Press, 2015.

———. *A Future for the Historical Jesus: The Place of Jesus in Preaching and Theology.* Nashville: Abingdon Press, 1971.

———. *Paul and His Letters.* Philadelphia: Fortress Press, 1988.

———. *Romans.* Nashville: Abingdon Press, 2005.

———. *Why Christ Matters Most: Toward a New Testament Christology.* Waco, TX: Baylor University Press, 2015.

———. *Who Is Jesus?: History In Perfect Tense.* Edinburgh: T&T Clark, 2001.

Knowles, Michael. *Jeremiah In Matthew's Gospel: The Rejected-Prophet Motif in Matthaean Redaction.* Sheffield: JSOT Press, 1993.

Kołakowski, Leszek. *God Owes Us Nothing: A Brief Remark on Pascal's Religion and on the Spirit of Jansenism.* Chicago: University of Chicago Press, 1995.

Kreider, Alan. *The Origins of Christendom in the West.* Edinburgh: T&T Clark, 2001.

Lane, William L. *Hebrews.* Dallas, TX: Word Books, 1991.

Le Van Baumer, Franklin. "The Conception of Christendom in Renaissance England." *Journal of the History of Ideas* (1945): 131–56.

Lüdemann, Gerd. *The Great Deception: And What Jesus Really Said and Did.* Amherst, NY: Prometheus Books, 1999.

Machen, J. Gresham. *The Origin of Paul's Religion.* New York: The Macmillan Company, 1921.

McLeod, Hugh, and Werner Ustorf. *The Decline of Christendom in Western Europe, 1750–2000*. Cambridge: Cambridge University Press, 2003.

MacMullen, Ramsay. *Christianizing the Roman Empire: (A.D. 100–400)*. New Haven: Yale University Press, 1984.

Malherbe, Abraham J., et al. *The Early Church in Its Context: Essays In Honor of Everett Ferguson*. Leiden: Brill, 1998.

Marsden, George M. *Understanding Fundamentalism and Evangelicalism*. Grand Rapids, MI: W.B. Eerdmans, 1991.

Martyn, J. Louis. *History and Theology in the Fourth Gospel*. Nashville: Abingdon, 1979.

Meinecke, Friedrich. *Historism: The Rise of a New Historical Outlook*. London: Routledge and K. Paul, 1972.

Morgan, Robert. "The Historical Jesus and the Theology of the New Testament," in James D.G. Dunn and Scot McKnight, eds., *The Historical Jesus in Recent Research*. University Park, PA: Penn State University Press, 2021: 567–84.

Morris, Jeremy. "The Strange Death of Christian Britain: Another Look at the Secularization Debate." *The Historical Journal* 46, no. 4 (2003): 963–76.

Nadel, George H. *Studies in the Philosophy of History*. New York: Harper and Row, 1965.

Nock, Arthur Darby. *Early Gentile Christianity and Its Hellenistic Background*. New York: Harper and Row, 1964.

Norris, Pippa, and Ronald Inglehart. *Sacred and Secular: Religion and Politics Worldwide*. Cambridge, UK: Cambridge University Press, 2004.

Novick, Peter. *That Noble Dream: The "Objectivity Question" and the American Historical Profession*. Cambridge: Cambridge University Press, 1988.

Passmore, John. "Explanation in Everyday Life, in Science, and in History," in George Nadel, ed., *Studies in the Philosophy of History*. New York: Harper and Row, 1965: 16–34.

Pauck, Wilhelm. *Harnack and Troeltsch: Two Historical Theologians.* New York: Oxford University Press, 1968.

Pauck, Wilhelm, and Marion Pauck. "Karl Holl" in their *From Luther to Tillich: The Reformers and Their Heirs.* San Francisco: Harper & Row, 1984: 139–45.

Ranke, Leopold von, and Georg G. Iggers. *The Theory and Practice of History.* London: Routledge, 2011.

Reill, Peter Hanns. *The German Enlightenment and the Rise of Historicism.* Berkeley: University of California Press, 1975.

Religionsgeschichtliche Volksbücher für Deutsche Christliche Gegenwart. Tübingen: J.C.B. Mohr, 1904.

Rémond, René. *Religion and Society in Modern Europe.* Oxford: Blackwell, 1999.

Rigney, Ann. *Imperfect Histories: The Elusive Past and the Legacy of Romantic Historicism.* Ithaca: Cornell University Press, 2001.

Rollmann, Hans. "William Wrede, Albert Eichhorn, and the 'Old Quest' of the Historical Jesus," in David J. Hawkin and Tom Robinson, eds., *Self-Definition and Self-Discovery in Early Christianity: A Study in Changing Horizons.* Lewiston: E. Mellen, 1990:79–99.

Rowland, Christopher, C. M. Tuckett, and Robert Morgan. *The Nature of New Testament Theology: Essays in Honour of Robert Morgan.* Malden, MA: Blackwell, 2006.

Rüsen, Jörn. "Rhetoric and Aesthetics of History: Leopold von Ranke." *History and Theory* 29, no. 2 (1990): 190–204.

Russell, James C. *The Germanization of Early Medieval Christianity: A Sociohistorical Approach to Religious Transformation.* Oxford: Oxford University Press, 1996.

Sandmel, Samuel. *Philo of Alexandria: An Introduction.* New York: Oxford University Press, 1979.

Schenck, Kenneth. *Cosmology and Eschatology In Hebrews: The Settings of the Sacrifice.* Cambridge: Cambridge University Press, 2007.

Schubert, Paul. "New Testament Study and Theology." *Religion in Life* 14 (1945): 556–71.

Segovia, Fernando F. *What Is John?* Atlanta: Scholars Press, 1996.

Smith, D. Moody. *John Among the Gospels.* Columbia, SC: University of South Carolina Press, 2001.

Smith, Gerald Birney. "The Religious Significance of the Humanity of Jesus." *The American Journal of Theology* 24, no. 2 (1920): 191–208.

Smith, Jonathan Z. *Drudgery Divine: On the Comparison of Early Christianities and the Religions of Late Antiquity.* London: School of Oriental and African Studies University of London, 1990.

Stern, Fritz. *The Varieties of History: From Voltaire to the Present.* London: Macmillan, 1970.

Strauß, David Friedrich. *The Christ of Faith and the Jesus of History: A Critique of Schleiermacher's Life of Jesus.* Philadelphia: Fortress Press, 1977.

Taylor, Charles. *A Secular Age.* Cambridge, MA: Belknap Press of Harvard University Press, 2007.

Troeltsch, Ernst. *The Absoluteness of Christianity and the History of Religions.* Louisville, KY: Westminster John Knox Press, 2006.

———. "Die Kleine Göttinger Fakultät von 1890." *Christliche Welt* 34 (1920): 281–3.

———. *Religion In History.* Minneapolis: Fortress Press, 1991.

Troeltsch, Ernst, and Gertrud Le Fort. *The Christian Faith: Based On Lectures Delivered at the University of Heidelberg in 1912 and 1913.* Minneapolis, MN: Fortress Press, 1991.

Veeser, H. Aram. *The New Historicism.* New York: Routledge, 1989.

Verheule, Anthonie F. *Wilhelm Bousset, Leben und Werk: Ein Theologiegeschichtlicher Versuch.* Amsterdam: Ton Bolland (voorheen H. A. van Bottenburg), 1973.

Wang, Q. Edward, and Georg G. Iggers. *Turning Points in Historiography: A Cross-Cultural Perspective.* Rochester, NY: University of Rochester Press, 2002.

Weiss, Bernhard. *Biblical Theology of the New Testament.* Edinburgh: T. & T. Clark, 1893.

Wessels, Antonie. *Europe, Was it Ever Really Christian? The Interaction Between Gospel and Culture.* London: SCM Press, 1994.

White, Hayden V. *Metahistory: The Historical Imagination in Nineteenth-century Europe.* Baltimore: Johns Hopkins University Press, 1973.

Wilken, Robert Louis. *The First Thousand Years: A Global History of Christianity.* New Haven: Yale University Press, 2012.

Windschuttle, Keith. *The Killing of History: How Literary Critics and Social Theorists Are Murdering Our Past.* New York: Free Press, 1997.

Winston, David, and John M. Dillon. *Two Treatises of Philo of Alexandria: A Commentary On "De Gigantibus" and "Quod Deus Sit Immutabilis."* Chico, CA: Scholars Press, 1983.

Wrede, William. *Über Aufgabe und Methode Der Sogenannten Neutestamentlichen Theologie.* Göttingen: Vandenhoeck und Ruprecht, 1897; translated in Robert Morgan, ed., *The Nature of New Testament Theology: The Contribution of William Wrede and Adolf Schlatter.* Naperville, IL: A. R. Allenson, 1973.

———. *The Messianic Secret.* Greenwood, SC: Attic Press, 1971.

Wrede, William, and Wilhelm Bousset. *Paulus.* Tübingen: J. C. B. Mohr (P. Siebeck), 1907.

Wright, N. T. *The Resurrection of the Son of God.* Minneapolis: Fortress Press, 2003.

Young, Frances M. *The Use of Sacrificial Ideas in Greek Christian Writers From the New Testament to John Chrysostom.* Cambridge, MA: Philadelphia Patristic Foundation, 1979.

Zager, Werner. *Liberale Exegese Des Neuen Testaments: David Friedrich Strauss – William Wrede – Albert Schweitzer – Rudolf Bultmann.* Neukirchen-Vluyn: Neukirchener, 2004.

SCRIPTURE INDEX

23:3 71
23:6 72
23:8–10 79
23:23–24 72
23:26 71
23:27–29 72
23:29–30 72
23:37 86
23:37–38 64
24:9–13 70
24:11–12 70
24:14 55
24:24 70
24:36 82
24:55 66
25:31–46 59
26:3–5 57
26:17 70
26:28 61, 80
26:31–35 80
26:40–46 80
26:47 57
26:54–56 56
26:56 65
26:59 57
26:63 67, 81
27:1 57
27:3 57
27:11–14 64
27:15–23 63
27:18 64
27:19 74
27:23–28 61

27:25 63
27:40 81
27:46 40
27:54 81
27:57 55
28:12–15 57
28:16–20 53, 54, 59
31:16 57
51:26 86

Mark
1:11 40
1:14 39
1:19–20 106
4:11–12 62
4:15 134
5:19 39
6:1 39
7:9 67
8:4 39
8:27–30 39
8:31–33 39
9:7 40
14:13–16 39
15:34 40

Luke
2:14–50 39
3:7–14 174n17
3:21 40
10:18 40
11:1 40